Toni Tennille
A Memoir

Toni Tennille
with Caroline Tennille St. Clair

TAYLOR TRADE PUBLISHING
Lanham • Boulder • New York • London

I dedicate this memoir, with love and a grateful heart, to my
father Frank and my mother Cathryn,
to my three sisters Jane, Louisa, and Melissa,
and to my niece Caroline

TAYLOR TRADE PUBLISHING
An imprint of Rowman & Littlefield

Distributed by NATIONAL BOOK NETWORK

British Library Cataloguing-in-Publication Information Available

Library of Congress Cataloging-in-Publication Data
Names: Tennille, Toni. | Tennille St. Clair, Caroline.
Title: Toni Tennille : a memoir / Toni Tennille with Caroline Tennille St. Clair.
Description: Lanham : Taylor Trade Publishing, [2016]
Identifiers: LCCN 2015042403 | ISBN 9781630761745 (hardcover)
Subjects: LCSH: Tennille, Toni. | Singers—United States—Biography. | Biographies. lcgft
Classification: LCC ML420.T328 A3 2016 | DDC 782.42164092—dc23 LC record available at http://lccn.loc.gov/2015042403

ISBN 978-1-63076-175-2 (e-book)

♾™ The paper used in this publication meets the minimum requirements of American National Standard for Information Sciences—Permanence of Paper for Printed Library Materials, ANSI/NISO Z39.48-1992.

Printed in the United States of America

CHAPTER 1

Montgomery, Alabama, 1946

THE HUGE STEEL WHEELBARROW CRASHED DOWN ON MY TINY index finger and nearly severed it at the joint. I lay on the floor of our neighbor's garage as my friends looked on in horror. Only seconds before we had been playing an innocent, silly game: We were running in and out of the narrow confines of the garage, chasing each other and laughing, when I slipped and knocked over the wheelbarrow. It crushed my finger to a bloody pulp.

What happened next is pretty much a blurred mix of my friend's mother hurrying to my side, being rushed to the hospital with what was left of my finger plunged into a glass of ice and water, and then being in the glaring light of an examination room. When the shock subsided, the pain took over. But what was almost worse than the pain was seeing the worried faces of my parents as they huddled by my bed, talking with the doctors. I knew that if the adults were this concerned, the accident must have been serious.

Despite the limits of reconstructive surgery in the 1940s, the doctors at our Montgomery hospital did everything they could to save my finger. But the end of my right index finger eventually succumbed to gangrene and had to be amputated. Being only five years old, I couldn't understand why the bandage on my index finger was shorter than the other fingers on my hand. When the doctors came in to examine it and change the bandages, I would always look away. Finally, I summoned up the courage to ask my parents why my index finger was shorter than the rest. With tears in their eyes, they gently explained what had happened.

I realize that many people would not think an incident like this was so terribly tragic. Children have accidents all the time—many far worse—and my life was never in danger. But even at such a young age, I had already begun to show promise of having musical talent, especially on the piano. Our family thrived on music—particularly my father—and they loved nurturing my growing passion for it. What would this accident—the partial loss of a finger—do to my budding music capability?

Determined to make the best of the situation, Mother and Daddy enlisted the services of a renowned New Orleans plastic surgeon, Dr. Neil Owen, to attempt to reconstruct my finger. We would make the three-hundred-mile drive down to New Orleans from Montgomery for what would end up being thirteen surgeries by Dr. Owen over several years. Those surgical procedures would prove to be long, painful ones in many ways. Ether, the primary anesthesia used for surgery in the 1940s, made me violently ill with nausea and vomiting when I woke up from a procedure. A piece of bone was removed from my hip to replace the finger bone that had been lost, and in order to encourage new skin tissue growth over the transplanted bone, my finger was sewn to an incision in my stomach for six weeks.

I have a photo that Daddy took of me during this phase. I'm smiling up at the camera from my hospital bed with my arm bandaged tightly to my waist to keep the finger in place where it is stitched to my stomach. Captured forever through the lens is Daddy's love and concern for his firstborn child and his determination to do whatever was needed to make things right—no matter the cost. Years later I realized that the numerous surgeries must have cost my parents an enormous amount of money—money that we probably didn't have. And later, when financial ruin finally caught up to our family, I felt guilty that the expenses from my accident had most likely contributed to it.

I experienced a tremendous amount of shame in the earlier stages of the reconstruction process when the finger still looked like a misshapen blob of fat and skin. It caused my classmates to shrink away in disgust, and a few even took it upon themselves to helpfully let me know my maimed finger was "ugly." In response, I began to craft a skill that I perfected throughout the rest of my life: hiding my finger. I learned to look people straight in the eye and give them a big, dazzling smile. After all, I reasoned, if they only looked at my face they wouldn't notice the finger!

Thinking back, this smoke-and-mirrors behavior probably benefited me later in life when I became a performer, because I learned early how to divert attention to the most positive parts of myself. Through those thirteen surgeries, Dr. Owen was able to shape my index finger into something that looked less "ugly," but it never again was a normal finger. I successfully hid this "flaw" from almost everyone for the rest of my life; I wore a stick-on nail during TV and concert appearances and deftly held my hand in certain ways so that it wasn't noticeable. Even some people who were very close to me never knew about it, or if they did, they never mentioned it. It was a secret that I carried with me everywhere, and I would know immediately if someone happened to look at my hand and notice something was wrong.

I was almost finished with the reconstructive surgeries when Mother took me for my first piano lesson with Miss Lilly Byron Gill. Miss Gill was a kind and gracious lady in her sixties who, in her youth, had studied with the famed composer and pianist Ignacy Paderewski. She taught her students in her Victorian-era house with long velvet drapes, sparkling chandeliers, and elaborate carved furniture, all of which whispered of faded grandeur from another time. Nervously, I showed my stunted finger to Miss Gill, worried about how she would react. To my relief she was completely undaunted and welcomed me as a piano student with open arms.

I wonder what would have happened if, instead of believing that I could overcome this slight handicap, Miss Gill had looked at my misshapen finger and told my parents to save their money—that I'd never be able play piano. If she had, my life would have been very different.

For years Miss Gill treated me as any other promising student and never, over the many years I studied with her, made me feel any less capable than if I'd had ten perfectly formed fingers. Under her tutelage, I grew into a very good classical pianist, knowing how to make my maimed finger work so that it didn't hamper my ability to play. I loved playing music for people, but I still never wanted them to see that the hands creating it were less than perfect.

In many ways, Montgomery, Alabama, still looks the same as it did when I lived there in the 1940s and '50s. Majestic magnolia trees still tower over the sidewalks in the neighborhood where we lived, scenting the air with their sweet, heady perfume; and just as they did decades ago, neatly trimmed azalea hedges continue to bank the foundations of lovely old homes. Our house on Felder Avenue looks so unchanged that I almost expect to see the front door fly open and me or my sisters scramble down the steps on our way to a lesson or to meet friends at the park.

But the Montgomery where I grew up was still clinging to the past; it was beaten, yes, but still defiant. Steadfast in old southern customs, the city was charged with racial tension, and it turned a deaf ear to the prophetic whisper of the civil rights movement only a decade away. Segregation ruled almost every aspect of life, from schools to hospitals and even bathrooms and water fountains. Although I didn't understand it at the time and accepted it as just "the way things were," I was always uncomfortable with segregation. My family would never utter a racial slur in public or private, and my sisters and I were taught to treat everyone, including our household help who were mostly black, with the same respect regardless of color. But even as a child, I couldn't help but notice the stark polarity between my community's black and white residents.

It was my father in particular who believed deep in his heart that all people, regardless of color, shared the same fears, hopes, and dreams. However, I suspect that when Daddy was around his "good ol' boy" friends, all of whom were quite prominent in Montgomery society, he would not openly protest their attitude toward our black citizens. They probably would have been appalled if they'd known Daddy's true feelings and might have even ostracized him, both socially and professionally. He was a businessman with a family to raise, so he did what he had to do. As children we were guarded by our parents from the true ugliness of segregation; in retrospect, I believe they were trying to protect us from what they themselves knew was wrong in our society.

My father, Frank, was a handsome man with an endearing smile, sparkling blue eyes, and a sweet tenor voice. He was just sixteen when his own father died and left the responsibilities of running the family furniture business to his mother, Edith. Edith managed the business until her health began to decline a few years later, when Daddy was in his early twenties.

At that time, Daddy had been on the cusp of a promising music career, touring all over the country with the Big Band circuit and singing as a solo act and with such luminaries as Bob Crosby and his orchestra, The Bobcats. I still have photographs of him onstage in front of the microphone, his face beaming with joy, surrounded by the orchestra, and resplendent in his tuxedo— a talented young man truly in his element. But he was the only son in the family, so when his mother's health began to fail and she needed him back home, he had no choice. Daddy packed his bags and went back to Montgomery, leaving behind the exciting world of a touring Big Band singer and, with it, his hopes and dreams of a music career. I know it broke his heart.

As his firstborn child, I believe that his passion for music was directly imparted to me. The Tennilles were a respected and socially prominent family in Montgomery with deep southern roots and even deeper secrets. My grandmother Edith loved her only son with an adoration that bordered on idolization. As she grew older, she began to depend on him heavily for emotional support. But my grandmother had even deeper troubles to which my father, from an early age, had been a helpless witness: She'd had a decades-long addiction to the strong opiate paregoric.

Paregoric was commonly used as a pain reliever in those days and, with a little manipulation, could be obtained from the pharmacist at the local drugstore. Eventually, Daddy became responsible for picking up bottles of the tinctures for his mother. My father later told me that he felt the pharmacists were charging my grandmother an inflated amount of money for the drug, knowing that, because she was an addict, she would pay it. Once when Daddy protested the price, the pharmacist fixed him with an icy gaze. "Now, Frank," he said. "You wouldn't want people knowing just how much paregoric your mother is using, would you?" At a very young age, he experienced the shame and stigma of addiction.

I know Daddy harbored a lifetime of guilt for his mother's pain because, when she gave birth to him, she suffered gynecological trauma that lasted the rest of her days. For a woman as proud as my grandmother, who would arrive for visits at our house in a chauffeured dark-blue Buick, this type of affliction must have been nearly unbearable. Self-medicating with opiates, while legal in the early twentieth century, was still something that people gossiped about. Who could blame her for using the one escape from chronic misery that was available across the drugstore counter?

Despite her addiction, I will always remember my grandmother as a dignified and immaculately dressed woman who adored her grandchildren. While my sister Jane and I were always excited to see Grandmother Edith arrive bearing her gifts of Madame Alexander dolls, candy, and crisp dollar bills, my mother was not. In the classic tug-of-war between the mother of an idolized only son and his wife, these two women competed for a place in Daddy's heart until my grandmother died when I was about seven, making Mother, by default, the winner.

My mother had been raised in a working-class home in Dallas, Texas. In my grandmother's narrow view, she was not socially suitable as a wife for her son. But when Daddy met young Cathryn Wright, who worked as a department store fashion model, her elegant beauty entranced him immediately. Despite his mother's disapproval, he and my mother married quickly, and Daddy took his lovely bride away from modern, bustling Dallas back home to Montgomery, the insular, provincial capital of the Old South. Perhaps my grandmother's early rejection of her instilled in Mother the resolute determination to prove her worth in the class-conscious culture in which she found herself. It was a challenge that Mother rose to with the zeal of a true champion.

Mother was perfect for the role as a privileged wife and Montgomery socialite; she was beautiful and charismatic, and she possessed exquisite taste. And my mother had some musical talent of her own. She and I would play duets together on the piano in the drawing room that she had decorated with chintz-covered sofas and classic pieces of furniture selected from Daddy's furniture store. While Daddy was always warm and affectionate, Mother was more reserved. I never doubted for a moment that she loved me, but she wasn't demonstrative in showing it.

Upon her arrival in Montgomery, Mother quickly rose through the social ranks and even served as president of the Junior League. She was proud of her charismatic husband and her pretty daughters but also very conscious of what other people thought. Her insecurity gradually grew into humiliation, as it became common knowledge that the "perfect" Tennille family was harboring a secret: My father was a binge alcoholic.

My father was frequently described as a man who "never met a stranger." Frank St. Clair Tennille loved being around people, and his magnetic personality made him the center of attention wherever he went. I can still see him striding through the

Tennille Furniture store on Bibb Street, charming customers with his warm salesmanship and joking with the staff, sharing a kind word with people of all walks of life and colors. While it was an unspoken rule in the Old South that blacks and whites did *not* socialize, Daddy threw convention to the wind every Labor Day when he hosted a huge picnic for the staff of the furniture store and their families.

The party was held in an open field on the outskirts of town, with the guests arriving in droves to relax, play games, and—most importantly—eat! On long gingham-covered tables, the women would set out a dazzling array of food. Platters of fried chicken, barbequed ribs, and sandwiches sat next to bowls of coleslaw and trays of baked macaroni and cheese. The dessert table sagged under the weight of home-baked pies, cakes, and cookies. Jane and I would run ourselves silly with the rest of the kids in the late-summer heat, stopping only to plunge our hands into the huge aluminum coolers filled with icy-cold soda pop or to raid the food tables. It was the one day we could eat and drink all we wanted, and no one, not even our eagle-eyed mother, would tell us we'd had enough.

Sitting together at tables in the shade of the huge oaks surrounding the field, families both black and white would share a picnic meal. And because Daddy's furniture store party was held in a remote field on the edge of Montgomery, out of sight from people who would not have approved, we were free to celebrate together a well-deserved day of rest and fun.

But Daddy's abuse of alcohol created a dark side to his normally sunny disposition. He would go weeks without a drink only to fall into the trap of "just one," which would lead him into the depths of another horrible binge period. At the time, alcoholism wasn't treated as the serious medical issue it is now. Addiction was something to be ashamed of and hidden away; when it couldn't be concealed, it became fodder for gossip among friends and neighbors.

My sisters and I adored our father, and it bewildered us to see him transform from the intelligent, industrious man we loved into a slurring drunk. Daddy was never mean when he drank—for which I am most grateful—but he would sometimes weep uncontrollably. My strong, capable father . . . would sob like a child! It made me angry to see him so weak. And it hurt our mother immensely. She was a proud woman, and Daddy's binges caused her to not only worry about his well-being but also about what was being said behind her back. My sister Jane and I tried to help by hiding Daddy's liquor from him or pouring it down the sink. Nothing ever did help, though, and Daddy's alcoholism ebbed and flowed like a poisoned river throughout our childhood. Mother wanted everything to be perfect: the beautifully decorated house, her tailored clothes, her talented, lovely family . . . and we almost were, except for Daddy's drinking. I have no doubt that my own lifelong penchant for perfection was forged by watching my mother desperately try to attain it in our home.

Much later in life, Mother told me that she almost called off her marriage to Daddy the day before the wedding. Maybe it was concern that her fiancé's drinking was more serious than she had thought; maybe it was the anxiety about leaving her family behind in Dallas. But all the plans had been set, the invitations had been sent, and a beautiful custom-made silk gown lay waiting for her, so there was, she reasoned, no way she could cancel. Mother put on the dress and met her groom at the altar, casting her misgivings aside as so many brides did before and have done since.

We are, as they say, simply the sum of our parts, and for almost everyone, the influence of a parent on those parts is the strongest of all. From my father I learned a deep love of music and the emotional power it wielded over both the player and the listener. He also honed my artistically critical eye through the hours we spent in his tiny garage darkroom, where I watched him skillfully develop the many family pictures he took.

Most precious of all, Daddy gifted to me the love of performing through his own talent as a singer and by introducing me to
the great music makers of the time. The Tennille home had the
finest hi-fi stereo in the neighborhood, and nothing delighted
Daddy more than sitting my sister Jane and me down in front
of it with a stack of records. "Listen right here, girls," he'd say,
pointing a finger in the air as Count Basie made the piano sing
jubilantly against the call and response of the horn section in his
orchestra. Frank Sinatra, Daddy taught us, was a master of pitch
and lyrical expression. Lying on my stomach on the carpet as Bil-
lie Holiday's velvety vocals poured from the speakers, I'd watch
my father close his eyes and smile as he savored the music. Listening to records was the time that I felt closest to him.

From an early age my mother, too, was an inspiration for
me. She possessed a keen intelligence and strong character and
wasn't afraid to voice her opinion in what was then very much
a "man's world," where women—especially southern women—
were expected to be deferential and meek. Watching her struggle
to keep the family together through the many years of my father's
alcoholism, I also learned the visceral skill of creating a veneer of
perfection when everything was, in truth, far from perfect. And
someday, just as she did as a young bride-to-be, I too would shrug
off that little voice telling me that my seemingly "perfect" relationship was, in fact, deeply and irrevocably flawed.

CHAPTER 2

IF YEARS FROM NOW SOMEONE WERE TO DISCOVER A BOX OF THE many black-and-white photographs my father took of our family, the person would not be faulted for assuming that the lives of the smiling individuals in the photos had been ones of a privileged and perfect happiness. Through his photography, he seemed to have endeavored to chronicle our family through the years, to capture and crystallize the happy moments that bubbled to the surface during our increasingly turbulent home life.

There is one photo of Jane and me posing proudly with my father next to our new Studebaker—we girls in matching plaid coats and knee-high stockings; Daddy grinning and dapper in his double-breasted overcoat and felt hat tilted to a slightly rakish angle. There is another of me squinting in the sun as I hold up a string of fish caught from Lake Martin, where we had a summer house. Daddy was very proud that his girls enjoyed spending hours fishing with him, and being the older sister, I was obligated to bait my own hook as well as my squeamish sister Jane's hook with wriggling catalpa worms. There are photos from our summer trips to the Florida panhandle, with Mother reclining in a chic black bathing suit and huge hat on the beach and us sitting happily on the sand by her side with big smiles and sunburnt noses.

Among Daddy's many candid shots, there are the beautiful formal portraits he loved to take, each carefully staged and lit to perfect the image of cultured family harmony. One I especially like was taken of my mother sitting on the bench at the grand piano in our home, holding my baby sister Louisa in her lap as Jane and I gathered at either side in our starched white dresses. Another, more relaxed in style, shows Jane and me on the chintz sofa with our elegantly dressed mother between us,

Vogue magazines stacked on the coffee table next to a silver bowl of flowers. The photos continued through the years as one more daughter, Melissa, was born. That made four Tennille sisters! Incredibly, when I now sift through all of the photos that documented our lives, I see not a trace of the darkness that sometimes eclipsed those happy, sunlit days.

Montgomery, like most southern cities in the 1940s and '50s, still rigidly held to the draconian rules of the past that dictated the rights of blacks versus whites. Schools, neighborhoods, and other centers of public life were segregated by race and were supposed to be "separate but equal." They were separate—but far from equal. But as a young girl, I wasn't completely aware of the social contradiction that defined where I grew up. Like most affluent whites, we always had black people working for us in our home, but to us they were more like part of the family.

When we weren't in school or playing in the backyard, my sister Jane and I loved to visit our father at the Tennille Furniture store. Founded by my grandfather in 1888, the store was located in a large brick building in the heart of downtown Montgomery. It had been a thriving family business and was a great source of pride for the Tennille family. As long as anyone could remember, the Tennille name had been pronounced Ten-*ill*. There are two small towns named after my ancestors—one in Georgia and one in Alabama—that are pronounced that way. When we later moved to California, Daddy decided to change the pronunciation of our name back to its original French version, Ten-*eel*. I think the decision to do so was a good one, since the French pronunciation is, in my opinion, much prettier.

My sister and I thought of the store as our own private playground, and we ran wild through it. It was the perfect place to play hide-and-seek with giant armoires to slip inside or tufted wingback chairs to duck behind. We would sneak into the Gallery, a beautifully styled salon that looked like a real room in a house. It was designed to show customers how the furniture looked when accessorized with matching drapes and pillows, and crystal decanters and silver bowls placed just so on the polished coffee tables. Jane and I would sit primly on the sofa in the Gallery pretending to drink tea and smoke cigarettes like fine society ladies, until a clerk would come along and shoo us out. We'd run to the back room where the seamstresses gossiped as they bent over the large whirring sewing machines, making custom drapes and slipcovers out of glazed cotton chintz and satin brocade fabrics. Sometimes they would let us rummage through their boxes of fabric scraps, and we'd each plunge our greedy hands in to find the best pieces before the other sister could grab them. Jane would make doll clothes from her scraps; I always made blankets for my beloved toy horse figurines.

But the inside of the store wasn't the only place where we liked to play. We would also hang out on the back dock, where the furniture was loaded onto the delivery truck. John and Fred, the two black deliverymen sang, laughed, and joked as they worked. We loved being out on the dock with them, although I have no doubt we probably got underfoot as they heaved furniture into the delivery truck. But Fred and John were always kind and patient, and they seemed to enjoy having us around.

There was, however, another part of the furniture store where Jane and I would sometimes venture, but always with a touch of trepidation. From the main floor, a large industrial elevator would make a creaky descent to the basement where extra inventory was stored. I never liked going into the basement. The low ceilings were painted black, and the space was dank and gloomy, with crates and cloth-covered furniture stacked on top of one another and just the narrowest of pathways to squeeze through. But something else in the basement bothered me even more than the looming shadows and ghostly shapes.

On the wall close to the elevator were two drinking fountains, side by side. The one on the right was a new model made of shiny stainless steel. It hummed as the internal motor cooled the water that spewed in a perfect arc from the spout when we pushed the button. Above it was a sign that said, "white." The one on the left was very old, probably put there when the store had been built. The porcelain basin was stained and had rust flaking from the metal pipes. This fountain had no motor and the water that flowed from the spout was lukewarm. The sign over this fountain read, "colored." Although we saw signs like this all over the city, from restaurants to public parks to movie theaters, it always bothered me to know that the right to have a cool drink of water on a hot Alabama day could depend simply on the color of a person's skin. When I think back to those drinking fountains, I can't help but wonder why Daddy, who truly appreciated his black staff, didn't bother to install a new "colored" fountain to match the one for whites. Although I'll never know his true thoughts on the matter, it very well could have been that Daddy never even noticed the disparity of the fountains the way that I did. He was a man from another time and place, a time riddled with inexcusable social inequalities but also a time when many people just accepted things the way they'd been for generations.

Mother and Daddy had an active social life, and many nights they would leave for an evening out to attend a party or have dinner with friends. They always looked so glamorous. I loved watching mother pause to look in the foyer mirror before she left, touching up her red lipstick or smoothing her dark hair. And no man ever looked more debonair than Daddy did in his beautifully tailored suit and silk tie. Mother, in her elegant dress and evening wrap, would always leave a cloud of Joy perfume wafting in the air as she went out the door, leaving Jane and me with our nanny, Denny.

Denny was the most special of all the many people who worked for us. She was with us for many years and became a beloved and important person in our lives. Thin and frail of body in her crisp white dress uniform, Denny's slight physique belied a strong but always gentle character. Denny was the first person for whom I ever really "performed." After baby Louisa had been tucked in her crib, Jane and I would sit Denny down on the couch and dim the lights, creating a dramatic stage presence in our living room. We'd put a record on Daddy's hi-fi and queue at the doorway until the first notes of music burst from the speakers. Then, wrapped in Mother's silk scarves and ropes of costume jewelry, we'd run into the room and perform an elaborate dance. Sometimes I was Odette, the tragic feathered princess in *Swan Lake*; other times I'd perform the more optimistic role of the Sugar Plum Fairy in *The Nutcracker Suite*. Jane and I fought for the spotlight, each jealously wanting all of Denny's attention, and sometimes the drama would rise to such a fever pitch that Denny would have to leave her seat to gently break up a fight between the dueling prima donnas. Denny was a receptive and brilliant audience of one, always clapping for more no matter how late into the evening these performances went.

On sunny days Denny would take Jane and me to Oak Park, a rambling city park with winding paths, swing sets, and a pond full of enormous goldfish that we could feed. To get to the park we'd have to board a city bus for the fifteen-minute cross-town trip. Once we'd climbed on and Denny had paid our fare to the driver and settled us on seats at the front of the bus, she would move to take her own seat at the back. Jane and I didn't like the idea of our Denny being away from us, and we'd sometimes leave our seats and go back to where she sat among the other black passengers. "No, no," she'd say. "You girls need to get back up to the front."

We couldn't understand why Denny had to sit in the back of the bus. It just didn't make sense. When we'd ask her why she'd answer, "Because that's just the way it is. Now go back up to the front." Sometimes—but only if the bus was empty—Denny would allow us to sit with her in the back. Only a few years later, in 1955, would a Montgomery seamstress named Rosa Parks decide that "that's just the way it is" wasn't a good-enough reason for her to keep standing on a crowded bus when seats in the "white" area were still open. Whatever Denny truly felt about segregated seating on the city bus, she didn't share it with us.

Denny's level-headed philosophy of childcare was a calming panacea in our often melodramatic young lives. There was one time in particular when I was about nine years old that her hands-on approach made a huge impact on me. We were at home with Denny, while Mother and Daddy were out, when I suddenly came down with a terrible headache. I went to my room to lie down, but the pain only got worse. I began to get hysterical, writhing in my bed with tears streaming down my face. Jane ran to get Denny. She came quickly and sat on the bed next to me, gently rubbing my arms and shoulders. "Shhh," Denny whispered. "Calm down now, child. Calm down." I remember her cool hands running over my brow and combing through my tangled hair. Then, just like that, the throbbing pain began to subside. When I opened my eyes, there was Denny holding something in her hand. "Miss Toni," she said. "What on God's green earth is your Momma's stocking garter doing wrapped around your head?"

Then I remembered that I had taken one of my mother's garters from her lingerie drawer and used it to pull back the hair off my face. The garter, made of rubber meant to hold up stockings on a lady's thigh, had created a tight constriction around my skull and cut off the flow of blood, which resulted in the agonizing headache. If Denny hadn't thought to run her fingers through my hair to soothe me, she'd never have discovered the garter, and I might have gone on suffering many more hours. It was just one example of Denny's loving and sensible approach to caring that made her so loved by all of us.

Years later, when Captain and Tennille were at the height of our career, we played a sold-out concert in Chicago where an elderly Denny had moved to live with her daughter. I arranged for a limousine to pick her and her family up and bring them to the venue, where they all had front row seats for the show. Nearly twenty-five years after Denny had applauded so rapturously for my childish dances in the living room, here she was again—still my number-one fan—among a crowd of thousands. After the concert, I was reunited with Denny, and as we embraced, I was filled with memories and emotion.

Some of my earliest and fondest memories from when I was young took place in our small kitchen with our cook, Estelle. She was a fantastic cook. When Daddy came back from quail hunting with his buddies, we'd watch as Estelle expertly removed the lead buckshot from the birds before cooking them in rich brown gravy inside a covered cast iron pot. We loved hanging around as she made shrimp creole with fluffy white rice or her famous cornbread, pulled crisp and hot from the oven in its own iron skillet. Always ravenous, Jane and I would prowl the kitchen like stray cats, sneaking bits of food behind Estelle's back until she'd finally decide she'd had enough and chase us out.

I also remember Lucille—light-skinned, large-boned, and unusually tall—who worked as our cook and housekeeper during the last years we lived in Montgomery. Lucille, like most of the help in Montgomery at that time, didn't own a car, so Daddy would drive her home each night. When I was old enough to drive, I happily took over this routine. Every night, Jane and I would chauffeur Lucille all the way to her small house on the muddy banks of the Alabama River on the other side of Montgomery. The house had peeling blue paint and a rickety front porch where members of her extended family would often be sitting when we pulled up.

As she stepped out of the car, Lucille would always turn to us and say, with a stern shake of her finger, "Now you girls lock these doors and go *right* on home!" Of course, we rarely would go straight home as we'd promised Lucille. With the exhilarating freedom of having the car to ourselves, we'd most often make a pit stop at the local Dairy Queen to buy Dilly Bars or take a turn through downtown before finally heading back home.

At the time I couldn't understand why Lucille was so afraid for our safety. I'm sure that some of it was just the general concern of a caregiver for her young charges. But I now realize that there was a more serious side to Lucille's apprehension, likely rooted in her awareness of the growing unrest within the black community. Beneath the manicured veneer of Montgomery life, with its clearly drawn lines between black and white, there simmered a hostile brew of social discontent. This anger would inspire a social revolution; it would start with lunch counter sit-ins and bus boycotts in the 1950s and, later, release a tidal wave of momentum for the civil rights movement throughout the South.

But at that time, things in Montgomery were still the same as they had been for almost a century, and as a young girl I didn't comprehend the seriousness of the growing turmoil. What Lucille saw and heard in her own neighborhood, where black people could safely express their anger without fear of reprisal, may have deepened her anxiety for the naïve Tennille girls who never thought for a moment that anything—or anyone—would bring them harm.

The chasm of racial inequality often manifested itself in surprising ways. One day when I was about fourteen, I went into the small bathroom off the kitchen, which was mostly used by Lucille and the other household help. I noticed something taped to the wall next to the toilet, and on closer inspection, I realized it was a page from a children's first-grade reader. On the page—probably torn from an old book that one of my younger sisters had discarded—were an illustration of a dog romping through grass and the words "See Spot run." It took me a moment to realize that Lucille must have taped the page to the wall so she could teach herself to read. I called Jane in to see it too. We were both sobered by the idea of a grown woman not knowing how to read. It was a watershed moment in my young life. Denny was from a middle-class family and had graduated from college, but Lucille, whose family was poor, was apparently not allowed the then-luxury of attending school. Even today the image of that faded page taped on the bathroom wall—and the quiet determination of a woman who just wanted to learn to read—remains vivid and poignant in my memory.

As the Tennille family grew in number, we moved into a succession of larger houses in the Montgomery area. Our first house, where we lived until I was sixteen, was a modest but smart-looking white clapboard home with dark-green shutters and pink azalea hedges. Although it was small, it was located in a desirable neighborhood. The backyard looked out over the Montgomery Country Club golf course, where Mother and Daddy played golf, a sport they both adored, with their friends. Sunday afternoons after church were spent at the country club, where lunch was served by a team of black waiters wearing immaculate white jackets with black bow ties. I'll never forget the delicious taste of the country club rolls, hot and fresh from the oven and set on the table in a basket wrapped in a white cloth. My sisters and I could never get enough of those rolls, devouring every one and "ruining our appetites," as Mother would say. When she was about four or five, my precocious little sister Louisa would run from table to table around the dining room, begging for rolls from other diners after our own table had run out. She was so adorable that she was never sent away empty-handed! Our exasperated Mother would usually send either Jane or me to fetch the wayward Louisa back to our own table. After lunch, the adults would smoke cigarettes and drink cocktails on the veranda while we kids raced around the manicured lawn or, when the weather was warm, splashed in the pool.

Until we moved to our last house on Felder Avenue when I was sixteen, Jane and I had to share a bedroom. For two very different personalities, such close proximity created a bit of animosity in our relationship. Jane was only twenty months younger than I was, but we had very different ideas about cohabitating; Jane was neat and I was, frankly, rather messy. My shelves were a riot

of books, magazines, and horse figurines, while Jane's were carefully lined with her dolls and stuffed animals. The carpet around
my bed was littered with clothes and shoes, while Jane's clothes
were hung neatly in the closet. In order to keep her side of the
room free of any mess from my side, Jane would stretch a string
across the room to clearly indicate the line of demarcation. This
procedure kept a wary peace until we moved and were able to
have our own bedrooms. Funny though, once we each got our
own room, Jane, no longer having to defend her territory, became
even messier than I was!

As the years went by music became an increasingly important
dynamic in my young life. Thanks to the encouragement of my
piano teacher, Miss Gill, who gave me the confidence to pursue piano despite the injury to my finger when I was five, my
desire for studying music only grew stronger. The first musical
instrument I'd tried was the violin, but I soon abandoned it when
I fell in love with the piano and learned how to read classical
music. Later in my career, that intensive classical training would
enable me to write my own music, something not every songwriter knows how to do. I also first played in front of an audience
at Miss Gill's, when her students were required to perform in the
music recitals she hosted in her home. You might think this was
an easy thing for a girl who loved to play music, but it wasn't.
Through all my years of performing in front of crowds, the only
time that I have ever experienced real stage fright was when I
played classical compositions at Miss Gill's recitals.

Waiting for my turn to play, I'd look out from the hallway
at the rows of chairs set up in the formal drawing room for the
spectators. There were Mother and Daddy, waiting patiently, and
beside them a very bored-looking Jane. A choking panic would
rise in my throat. What if I got up to the piano and couldn't
remember the notes? I could read music well, but at recitals,
the music sheets were not in front of you. You had to *memorize* the entire song. There I'd be in my best organdy dress and

patent-leather shoes, sitting in front of friends and family, unable to play a single note! They all might laugh at me, and the shame would be unbearable.

This internal agony would churn until the moment my name was called and I stepped forward to take my seat at the piano. My hands would tremble as they poised over the keys, and my feet would shake against the pedals. There were times when the anxiety was so overwhelming that I would swear I had actually blacked out and only came to as my fingers finished the piece. Through it all, somehow my hands always knew which notes to play even though my mind had been paralyzed by fear. Years later, including the times I stood waiting to walk onto a stage in front of thousands of people, nothing was ever as terrifying to me as my performances in Miss Gill's drawing room.

CHAPTER 3

IN 1952, WHEN I WAS TWELVE, THE FOURTH AND LAST TENNILLE daughter was born. Melissa was a beautiful baby with the same large blue eyes as our father and a sweet, calm demeanor. Denny would often say that Melissa was the "easiest" of the sisters, and I have no doubt she was right because our baby sister was often smiling and seldom cranky like the rest of us frequently were. Melissa was like our very own living doll, toddling over the lawn and screaming in delight as her dutiful older sisters chased behind to catch her when she tumbled down.

With such a large and active family, the house was always bustling with activity. The door would swing open and close with a bang as people went in and out all day. Jasmine curled around the back porch, infusing the summer air with its heady scent, as Lucille bustled about in the kitchen preparing dinner and humming along to the gospel station on her small radio. Sometimes a man would come to the back door, and Lucille would wipe her hands on her apron and go out to give him money. She called him a "policy man"; the small payments were for her burial insurance. I always felt uncomfortable as I watched Lucille count out her hard-earned money to these men, who were always white. I just hope that Lucille, when her time came, eventually did get the dignified funeral—in church with a good casket and lots of "going home" music—that she so wanted and very much deserved.

Daddy was an excellent golfer. Mother never became very good at the game, but she liked being outdoors and socializing with her women friends as they played the course at the country club. In the spring of 1955, Mother and Daddy were invited to be the emcees at a golf tournament the club was hosting, which was going to be covered live on WSFA-TV, an affiliate of NBC television. They were both thrilled and excited at the opportunity. During the coverage of the tournament, Mother worked the crowds, interviewing golfers and other prominent local attendees. She was wonderful! Mother was confident and gracious, and it showed. The questions came easily for her, and she showed an interest in each person she talked with. And she looked *fabulous*. I always knew that she had been a model before she married Daddy, but television truly captured her animated beauty as well as her lovely voice with its soft, southern accent. After the golf tournament, Mother was invited to meet with Hoyt Andres, the manager of the station, to discuss the possibility of a position. When she was offered a job doing interviews on television, she quickly accepted. I'm sure she was also thinking that this could help address the financial woes our family was beginning to experience.

The program, called *The Guest Room*, was at first just fifteen minutes long. But Mother quickly became a local celebrity, and the show time was increased to thirty minutes, Monday through Friday, and scheduled in the prime spot just before the local news, which was then followed by NBC national news. While my talent for music is undoubtedly a gift from my father, it is Mother who taught me the art of confidence in front of the camera, and even more important, how to make your guests feel at ease.

From the small set decorated with a sofa, a few armchairs, and a coffee table, Mother interviewed everyone from local politicians to writers and sports pros. Occasionally she'd snag a celebrity who happened to be traveling through Montgomery. It was incredibly exciting to visit the television station and watch the show being filmed live, as most television shows were in that day. Mother also had to do the commercials for products sponsoring the show. Any slip of the tongue or mistake Mother made couldn't be "done over," but the few times she flubbed a name or a word, she'd smoothly recover and continue the segment without missing a beat. Television was still very much a man's world when

Mother started her show; the only other woman who had her own program on local television at the time was Idelle Brooks, who had an exercise show. I got my first paying "gig" playing piano for Idelle's show while she cheerfully counted out leg lifts and toe-touches to the people exercising along with her at home.

Taking on so public a role as a television host without a hint of hesitation is just one example of how strong and adventurous Mother was. About four years after World War II had started, when I was about five and Jane was just three, Daddy was drafted into the Marine Corps and was quickly sent to the Pacific. As you can imagine, Mother and Daddy missed each other terribly. Never one to be patient, Mother made up her mind to drive all the way from Alabama to San Diego, California, to meet Daddy during the brief period of time when his ship would be back in San Diego for a few days. This was a journey of about four thousand miles round trip, back when there were no cell phones, interstate road systems, and many other conveniences we have today. Many women at the time wouldn't even drive across city lines without a male escort, much less with two small children, but Mother was a different kind of woman. Not being entirely crazy though, she made the wise decision to hire a nanny to help watch Jane and me while she drove. It would be perfect, she thought.

Virgilee, a young black woman unencumbered by marriage or children, was quickly recruited for the expedition. Pretty and slender as a gazelle, Mother used to say that Virgilee was "footloose and fancy-free." Eager to see some of the world beyond Alabama, Virgilee would be the ideal traveling companion. There was the problem of finding places to eat or rest along the way, for many of the states we passed through were still segregated, and the "white" motels and restaurants would not welcome Virgilee. But somehow, mother managed to drive the four of us across the country to San Diego. I don't know how she did it, but she did. There was one delay on the drive out when one of the tires on our

car blew out in Texas, and we had to wait for the ration committee to meet and approve a new one for us. This was wartime, and
rubber, along with many other things, was in short supply. Thankfully, the committee decided that a young mother stuck out in the
middle of the country with two children and a young maid was a
good enough reason to qualify for a tire, so we were able to make
the rest of the trip.

I was too young to absorb many details of the trip, but in my
mind's eye I can still see the dusty car roaring through the open
plains of the Midwest or winding through the red canyons of
New Mexico. My sister and I are in the backseat, our sleepy heads
resting against Virgilee's shoulder, and Mother is at the wheel in
her silk headscarf and sunglasses.

We were so glad to see Daddy after many months of sepa-
ration, and we all spent happy days together at a lovely resort
by the sea called Casa de Manana. In addition to his duties as
an aide to the venerable General "Howling Mad" Smith, Daddy
also sang with "The Merry Men of the Marines," a group that
performed over the radio for the troops. I remember the wonderful young men who were in the troupe coming by to visit our
bungalow; there were dancers, musicians, and even an acrobat!
Mother and Daddy were so in love, and for a while, even in the
midst of a devastating world war, everything seemed right in our
little world.

Years later, Mother told me that the time in California went
by so fast that she dreaded the thought of having to drive all
the way back to Alabama. But Daddy was preparing to leave,
and money was running out. After saying a tearful good-bye to
Daddy and seeing him off on the ship with the rest of his regi-
ment, we returned to our hotel to pack for the long trip back to
Montgomery. You can just imagine the shock and dismay that
Mother experienced when we got there and found a handwritten
note by the telephone. It was short and sweet:

Dear Mrs. T,
I am staying in California. Good-bye.
Virgilee

Evidently, Virgilee had decided that she wouldn't be going back to Montgomery after all. Mother would have to do the long drive and keep an eye on us kids all by herself. When Jane and I were older and the California trip would come up in conversation, she would throw her hands up in the air with exasperation about Virgilee abandoning us to stay behind. But then she would smile and say, "But you know, I could hardly blame her. There sure wasn't much hope for an ambitious, young black woman in Montgomery." I wonder sometimes whatever happened to Virgilee. I hope she stayed safe and had a good, happy life in her new home.

As profits from the Tennille furniture store began to slow, Mother's paycheck brought in much-needed income for our large family. Times were changing; people began to move from cities into outlying suburbs, and their shopping dollars went with them. Air-conditioned, indoor malls drew thousands away from the downtown stores that had thrived for almost a century. It probably was no help that Daddy was not an astute business-man. Instead of meeting the demands of the average Montgomery family's furniture needs and budget, he sourced the kinds of things he loved. The store was filled with elegant, expensive pieces from Baker and Drexel, brands that only a small percentage of the local population could afford. Often the best pieces went unsold and would eventually make their way into our house. It was like a well-appointed house of cards, lovely to look at but all too fragile in the winds of a changing economy.

One of the early signs of our impending financial troubles happened when I was in the fifth grade. With her eyes full of regret, Mother sat Jane and me down and told us that we would no longer be able to attend the private school where we'd both gone since kindergarten. Housed in an old mansion downtown,

Margaret Booth School was a fine Montgomery institution for young girls and ladies. Far from being the stereotypical southern girls' school concerned only with table manners and serving tea, Margaret Booth School was renowned for having the rather modern philosophy that a girl's education should be just as good as a boy's. The classes were very small with no more than seven or eight students in each, so we received a lot of individual attention. Always a studious girl who enjoyed school, I loved the formal routine and discipline taught to the small student body where the curriculum included advanced mathematics, music, and French conversation. Here I was able to meet and make friends with girls from other cultures, daughters of Montgomery's distinguished Greek and Jewish families who, despite their education and prestige, were not welcome at our Waspy country club.

Every school day would begin with a brief assembly in a large room on the first floor where we would all gather to be greeted by the intellectual and enigmatic Madame Booth herself. She would proceed to update us on any recent or upcoming happenings at the school, and when she was finished, we students would close the assembly by singing the school's Alma Mater, accompanied on the piano by one of the senior students. I loved the singing and being close to the sophisticated older girls in their matching cardigan sweaters and pearl necklaces. Someday, I daydreamed, maybe I would be sophisticated and "all grown up" just like them.

But Margaret Booth school tuition was expensive. Although Mother was contributing to the family income with her small salary from the TV show, the furniture store was losing money every year. There wasn't enough left over to afford the luxury of private school. I know it hurt both Mother and Daddy to take us out of the wonderful school both Jane and I loved so much, but there was no choice. We started the following year at the public grade school, Cloverdale, and after getting used to the idea that I now shared a classroom with boys, I happily settled into my new—if quite different—academic setting.

It seemed for a while that our lives were settling down. The "crisis" periods were farther apart and Daddy's drinking sometimes seemed like a series of bad dreams in the past. Mother was busy with her TV show and Daddy, who had been elected to the Alabama legislature, became the moderator of a weekly television show called *The Legislature Speaks* on WCOV, another local station. I continued piano lessons with Miss Gill while immersing myself in study and extracurricular activities. Being in school offered me challenges that helped me put aside, for a time, the anxiety of Daddy's alcoholism.

Mother understood how much I dreaded another summer with no school commitments and activities to keep me busy and give me a reason to be away from home. After thorough investigation, she decided that I should go to summer camp at Camp Illahee in North Carolina. When I learned that the camp was "all about horses," I was thrilled! The summer after I turned fourteen, I set off for one blissful month of canoeing, riflery, horseback riding, and singing around the campfire. I remember one evening all the girls gathered by the lakeshore and placed lit candles inside tiny paper boats. Then, as the illuminated vessels caught the wind and drifted away like dancing fireflies, we sang together: "Baby's boat's the silver moon, sailing in the sky, sailing on a sea of sleep, while the clouds float by." It was a wonderful and happy experience that I will always cherish.

Shortly after I returned home from camp, I realized that nothing had changed. There was still tension bristling between Mother and Daddy. She was very busy with her new career and had little time to devote to him, and my father needed a lot of attention. Despite our constant financial worries, they were able to purchase a larger home in an older section of Montgomery on Felder Avenue. Finally, Jane and I would get our much-coveted separate bedrooms! Both of us started packing right away when we heard the news. But before we could move in, Daddy entered another period of binge drinking. Our excitement over the new house, and with it the hope for a tranquil future, was crushed.

Looking back, I can see now that Daddy was depressed—depressed by the failing family business his grandfather had founded and the pressure to support our family in the way to which we were accustomed. I'm sure he was also ashamed because our Mother was now predominantly the breadwinner of our family. Still, I was so angry with him when he drank. I was embarrassed knowing that other people were whispering about him. I despised the sound of the beer bottle opening and the way he slurred his words. But the worst was the incessant crying.

By the crying stage, Mother would have already had her terse words with Daddy and left with a slam of the door in disgust. The help would slip discreetly into the kitchen, tight-lipped, exchanging knowing looks and barely perceptible shakes of their heads. I'd stand in the doorway to the living room and watch as he hung his face in his hands and wept so that the tears slipped through his fingers. *Why?* I would think angrily. *Why are you doing this to Mother? Why are you doing this to us?* I didn't understand that this condition that caused Daddy to drink so heavily was a disease, and even if I had at the time, I'm not sure it would have changed my feelings much.

Perhaps when he was sitting at his desk amid overdue bills and dwindling sales receipts, the heartache of that long-ago abandoned dream of being a performer would come back to haunt him. Maybe drinking was the only way to banish those memories and ease the stress of middle-aged life. I suppose, in retrospect, we were lucky that our father was never, ever a violent drunk. But his drinking binges, although sporadic with months of sobriety in between, were emotionally traumatizing. They wrecked the momentum of our lives like a boat that steams across calm waters and suddenly, out of nowhere, hits an iceberg, throwing everyone on board off balance. *What would happen to us,* I sometimes wondered, *if he didn't stop drinking?*

Jane and I had different ways of dealing with Daddy when he drank. While she hated the turmoil it created just as much as I did, Jane was Daddy's buddy and wanted to defend him. Mother would sometimes bring home a six-pack of beer and tell Daddy, "This is all you get today, Frank. So make it last." Jane would carefully dole out a few sips to him at a time and then run to the kitchen to put the bottle back in the refrigerator to keep it cold, thereby "making it last longer." Our entire family was caught in the web that alcohol abuse can weave. There are no winners, just survivors, in this game.

Daddy's drinking came to a head when I was about fifteen. He fell headlong into a binge so intense that he went missing for a week. "Frank Tennille Presumed Dead!" the headlines in the Montgomery newspaper shrilled, setting off a torrent of gossip that our father had been murdered or had run off with another woman. It was a surreal time, with Mother trying to hold her head up amid the whispers and go to work while also managing the household. Daddy was eventually found at a motel in Florida by Bummy, a good friend with whom he had attended Alcoholics Anonymous meetings. "Frank Tennille Found in Florida Suffering from Amnesia!" the newspaper shouted with undisguised glee. It was obvious to everyone that Daddy had finally reached rock bottom and he seriously needed help. He would have to stop drinking cold turkey and go through the dreaded DTs—detoxification. Bummy helped make arrangements for him to go to St. Jude's Hospital in Montgomery. At the time St. Jude's was a "colored" hospital, but they agreed to accept him, knowing how desperately he needed help. That hospital and its devoted staff saved my father's life. Daddy continued to drink until he finally became sober after our move to California, but he never had another binge like the one that could have claimed his life.

Once Daddy came home from the hospital, we were able to move into our new house. Although we now had our own rooms,

Jane and I would still spend hours together poring over Mother's copies of *Vogue* and other fashion magazines. We'd each pick a "side" of the same magazine and would take turns commenting and critiquing the fashions featured on our respective pages as we flipped through. We also loved playing records and listening to the radio. The local black music station, WRMA, was where I learned to love rhythm and blues, doo-wop, and boogie, all sounds that were steadily gaining momentum on airwaves all over the country. It was an exciting time for a young girl who loved music. The jubilant pomp of Fats Domino, Chuck Berry, and Elvis Presley infiltrated the radio waves with a sound filled with sexual exuberance and a youthful—if sometimes defiant—charisma. This new music frightened many older people who considered it rebellious and even immoral, but to us teenagers—black and white alike—it nudged something in our souls and made us want to dance like nothing else.

Entering high school offered many ways for me to escape the turmoil at home. Always a good student, I became vice president of the Latin Club, sang in the Glee Club, and worked my way up through trigonometry. I always had friends, but I wasn't considered "popular." Already taller than many of the boys in my class, I had yet to become comfortable with my ungainly height that would eventually reach five feet eleven inches. Jane, on the other hand, was growing into a head-turning young beauty with amber eyes set under the dark brows she inherited from our mother. Although she was lovely and well liked, Jane always seemed a bit shy as a teenager. She walked the halls of our school in a brown swing coat with a velvet collar that I swear she hardly *ever* took off. I now wonder if Jane wore that coat as a kind of unconscious armor to guard against the tumultuous home life that we shared. My sister and I were very different when we were growing up—Jane was dreamy and a little wild, while I was studious and reserved—but we were always, and still are to this day, there for one another at a moment's notice.

Daddy was as proud as a father could be when I was accepted to Auburn University at the end of my senior year in high school. Once there, he was certain, I'd finally meet a tall, southern-bred, sports-loving man and marry him. Then Daddy would finally have a son. In those days women went to college to find a husband; academic achievements were considered secondary. But I was excited at the prospect of going to college and furthering my music studies. Finally, I'd be out of boring old Montgomery and free to explore a whole new world—albeit one that was just two hours away from home. I could leave behind the anxiety of wondering when Daddy would drink again as well as the pressure of the financial turmoil that loomed over our house. In the fall of 1958, I packed up my best skirts, blouses, and sweater sets and piled into the car with Mother, Daddy, and Jane for the trek east on Highway 80 to the leafy college town of Auburn, Alabama.

The Montgomery I left behind that sultry Indian summer day was beginning to strain at the rusty shackles of its segregated past, the links slowly breaking with each succession of social movements buoyed by the Civil Rights Act of 1957. Buses in the South were now desegregated, but the precarious and sometimes bloody path to racial equality still loomed ahead. Since much of the white South remained defiant to the changes laid down by federal courts, the injustices of the past went on, like a Confederate fiddler playing long after the dance floor has emptied. Auburn University, which had only begun accepting women a few years before I enrolled, was still a white college when I arrived as a freshman and wouldn't see its first black student until 1964.

I didn't know it at the time, but by then I'd be long gone from Alabama.

CHAPTER 4

MY MOTHER HAD ALWAYS WISHED FOR ME TO GO TO AN ESTEEMED women's college like Vassar or Smith. While I certainly had the grades to get into one of those institutions, there was no question that Frank Tennille's oldest child would attend none other than his beloved Auburn University. Even if Mother had managed to get her way, there would not have been enough money to afford the steep tuition for an exclusive private college. As it turned out, there was not even enough money to keep me in Auburn for more than two years. But the fall that I first arrived on Auburn's red-bricked campus, the financial and personal worries of my family seemed far behind in Montgomery. I was finally on my way to true independence.

Some of that independence was held in check by the strict— and often sexist—standards to which female students were held. We were not allowed to wear shorts or pants anywhere on campus. Girls walked around campus in their swingy skirts with sweater sets and pearls like proper young ladies. The girls' dormitory was watched over by a resident housemother who took her job of guarding her virginal charges quite seriously. She would stand at the door checking off names for the ten p.m. curfew, sniffing for any trace of alcohol after we returned from an evening out. Men, of course, were not allowed upstairs in the girls' dorm at any time. They had to wait for their dates or friends in the common area downstairs, always under the watchful eye of the housemother.

But despite these puritanical measures, sometimes our raging co-ed hormones would boil over into a strange collegiate ritual known as a "panty raid." The first tremors of an impending attack would come with whispers among the girls that a certain group of young men were planning a "raid." There would be shrieks of excitement and giddy anticipation up and down the halls of the girls' dorm as the male students began to gather outside. Then, when the tension was almost to a bursting point, the men would start to chant: "Throw down your panties!" Of course, we fair blossoms were safely locked inside the dorm, but that didn't stop some of the more affected girls from flinging their undergarments out the window to the boys on the ground below. I found this behavior completely silly and kept all my underpants where they belonged—in my dresser drawer!

Mother strongly felt that I should join a sorority, so I gamely went through the motions of "rush" week, in which the various sororities on campus opened their doors to new prospects, looked them over, and selected the ones they wanted. I never felt very comfortable with sorority life, with its emphasis on social status and wearing the "right" kinds of clothes, but when Delta Delta Delta extended an invitation to me, I accepted. Although many of my fellow "sisters" were lovely girls, it gradually became apparent that I just didn't have much in common with them. Somehow, despite my lukewarm interest in being a sorority girl, I was nominated by the chapter to be their candidate for Miss Auburn. I never had viewed myself as being exceptionally pretty, but I was statuesque and blonde with a big smile, and that must have been enough to qualify as a college beauty queen. I didn't win the crown, but just being selected as a finalist made me realize that I was no longer the tall, gawky girl the boys didn't notice.

The sexual tension on campus was not surprising because, in 1959, male students outnumbered women students about four to one. There was never a shortage of fellows eager for a date, and Daddy did his part by quickly introducing me to the Auburn football and basketball players he'd made the acquaintance of at the many alumni events he'd attended. During my awkward adolescent years, he had always assured me that college would be the place where I would "blossom." A nice basketball player, tall enough to not feel intimidated by my height, would be just the

ticket for a dreamy college romance and maybe even an engage-
ment ring. For a "nice" young southern girl in 1959, finding a husband was supposed to be more important than earning a degree.

While I wasn't too anxious to snag a ring, the idea of finding a soul mate among the many young men on campus had its
appeal. The well-bred, sporty young men Daddy tried to match
me with were among the most eligible on campus, but they were
not the ones who attracted me. I liked boys who were sensitive
and mysterious, like many of the jazz musicians I idolized. I
already knew that any soul mate of mine would *never* be a ball-
throwing jock—sorry, Daddy!

Like so many young students, I wasn't exactly sure what I
wanted to do after college. Since I'd always loved to read, I set my
sights on an English degree, with the eventual goal of teaching
literature and poetry. But I soon realized that before I could teach
the nuances of Emily Dickinson or dissect the themes in Shake-
speare's plays to a classroom full of students who loved literature
as much as I did, I'd first have to put in years of instructing reme-
dial English to bored football players! Knowing I would not be
able to stomach such an assignment, I turned my focus to music.
Not only did I hone my entertainment skills in the classroom, but
in the workplace too, because I landed *the* perfect job right there
on campus. The perfect job for a girl who loved to sing—and who
also loved musicians!

The Auburn Knights Orchestra, started by a small group
of student musicians in the early 1930s, had grown into a full-
fledged big band of sixteen musicians by the time I arrived at the
college. By the '50s it had the reputation of being one of the most
accomplished dance orchestras in the South, playing campus
social events, cotillion balls, country club functions, and dance
parties. Daddy had been the Knights' very first vocalist when he
was an Auburn student, so we were both bound and determined
that I would follow in his footsteps and be the second Tennille
to sing with the band. Before I had even unpacked my trunk in

the tiny dorm room I shared with another girl, I found myself auditioning for the coveted role of the female singer—the only one in the whole orchestra. After so many years singing along with Daddy to his favorite Woody Herman and Ella Fitzgerald records, I was finally ready to add my own voice to a real live band. And I got the job!

Singing in front of those rapturous horns, hip-swaying drums, and rollicking piano notes made me feel truly alive. Also, I was grateful for the little bit of money I earned as a Knight to help fund my modest living expenses, because I knew that things were still very tight at home. But what I learned from performing with the Auburn Knights paid me far more than any amount of money could have. That musical experience combined with my classical-music education provided the tools I would need when I began writing my own songs. My childhood training gave me the ability to play piano and read music. The guys in the Knights taught me how to read and write chord symbols and make lead sheets. In classical music, you play what is written—exactly as it is written—with no improvisation. With jazz or pop, you have the freedom to experiment with the melody or the rhythm and "personalize" the music you create.

Because the orchestra was in high demand for dances and social events all over the South, many weekends we'd have to travel out of state for gigs. Our mode of transportation was a dilapidated old Cadillac hearse that someone had painted pink, and a bunch of us would crowd together on makeshift bench seats for the trip while the band manager followed with all the instruments crammed in his car. On really long drives, I'd sneak off campus in my forbidden jeans and then, once we'd arrived at the venue, I would struggle into my fancy stage dress in the back of the old hearse before going onstage—much to the amusement of my male band members. Sometimes we traveled in an old band bus fitted out with bunk beds in the back where I could at least stand up straight while I dressed.

It was in one of these bunk beds where I lost my virginity to our alluring, dark-eyed lead trumpet player whom I'll call "Johnny." While the other musicians were boisterous and loud, Johnny was mysterious and reserved, and I developed a huge crush on him. I'm not sure exactly how the two of us ended up in that bus bunk one night after a late gig, but we did, and I decided he was the one I'd "give myself" to. Instead of the deep, romantic encounter I'd always imagined, the experience was awkward and uncomfortable! After that night I was sure Johnny thought of me as a "bad" girl and would want nothing more to do with me, so I avoided him at all costs. Besides, we hadn't used any protection—no one knew anything about birth control in those days—so I spent the next few weeks worrying I might be pregnant until, thankfully, I got my period. Decades later, after one of my big-band performances, a man came up to me and introduced himself. It was Johnny! My mysterious, cool-cat trumpet player had grown up and become, of all things, a CPA.

My role in the orchestra made me the one girl in my dorm with a legitimate excuse for not making curfew. Some nights we'd get back so late that the band manager and I would have to search for the night watch guard so he could unlock the dorm for me to get in. Sometimes we'd wander all over campus in the wee hours of the morning, totally exhausted, until we finally found him. Eventually I got permission to live off campus and could come and go as I pleased. Not that I took advantage of this freedom—I was still sort of a "square" girl, and most of the band treated me like a sister! Once I was out of the dorm, I stopped attending sorority functions too. I was much more interested in hanging out with the cool, artsy crowd—poets, musicians, and actors. Our favorite hangout was Toomer's Corner, a pharmacy near campus with a small restaurant in the back where we'd drink coffee and talk for hours, laughing and arguing over art, music, and life. Between discovering the meaning of existence with my new friends and performing with the Auburn Knights, interest in some of my less creative classes waned. I still excelled in literature and music, but my grades in physics and zoology dipped lower and lower as the semester went on.

As if I didn't already have enough to do, I joined the Concert Choir, a group dedicated mostly to classical compositions, and the Women's Jazz Octet, which was founded by Professor Bob "Fop" Richardson. We sang original jazz-styled arrangements, mostly written by Professor Richardson. Each arrangement was both an adventurous vocal challenge and just flat out fun! I have always loved singing and harmonizing with other singers to create the glorious sound that only blended human voices can make.

Between classes and my music activities, there wasn't much free time to go back home for visits, but I saw my family when they drove over from Montgomery to attend Auburn football games. Louisa was quickly growing from a child into a tall and slender adolescent; little Melissa was now our only "baby," with her bright smile and laughing blue eyes. There was a chilly tension between Mother and Daddy even when they tried to act as if everything was fine. I knew it wasn't; our financial situation had become too dire to ignore any longer. One rare weekend when I was home, Mother sat me down and told me that the family furniture store was being sold. We were so far in the hole that even the sale of the store wouldn't be enough to cover our debts. Collectors would phone incessantly trying to find Daddy, and one of my sisters would have to lie and say he wasn't home. That alone was a shock, but what she said next really floored me. The family was leaving Montgomery—our home for all my life—and moving out to California.

Mother explained that there was no future for Daddy in Montgomery any longer. A distant Tennille relation and family friend, Alex Burton, was a VP at North American Aviation in Los Angeles. He had recommended Daddy for a customer relations job with the company in their Autonetics division and, while the salary wasn't particularly high, it was enough to help get the family back on its feet. It would mean a whole new life for everyone, an opportunity for Daddy to start over fresh and gain back some of the pride he'd slowly lost over the years of debt and drinking.

Of course, moving meant that Mother would have to give up her television show, and I know that hurt her deeply. She had worked hard to develop and refine her on-air career for many years, and now it would all be gone. But she still had young children to think about and was willing to make the sacrifice if it meant keeping the family together. And just maybe, Mother and I both thought without actually saying it, the adventure of creating a home in a new place would be the balm to heal my parent's tattered marriage. Maybe there was still hope to recover the deep love they had once felt for each other.

I went back to Auburn with a heavy heart, knowing that my entire family would soon be moving across the country. Sure, I'd been enjoying my time away from the family, but their presence just a couple hours' drive away had always been comforting. I busied myself with singing, friends, and classes. But as summer break approached, my apprehension grew into excitement. Daddy had already left for California, taking Jane with him so she could start her senior year at her new high school. Mother was finishing up the packing and would follow with the rest of the family as soon as the house was sold. Once classes were over, I would be making the long flight from Alabama to California to join them for the summer.

Daddy had gotten Jane and me jobs at Autonetics, which was very exciting since I'd never had a "real" job except singing or playing the piano. The thrilling anticipation of a new life out west increased when Jane called to report on our rented house in New-port Beach; there were palm trees in the yard and boys walking by carrying surfboards to the beach—which was just across the street!

I remember so clearly that when the plane began to descend, I was amazed by the massive clusters of lights that emerged through a veil of clouds. Some lights were tucked deep inside valleys like a thousand netted fireflies and others were sprinkled along the tops of mountains, beyond which the dark expanse of the Pacific lay like a deep void. Never in my life had I seen so many lights; each one illuminating the lives of people with their own hopes and dreams, just like me! For the first time I realized how huge the world really was, and that soon, in some way, I would be finding my place in it.

The new family home on East Ocean Boulevard was much smaller than we were used to, but it made up for lack of size in sheer character and location. It was Spanish-style with pink painted stucco and a red tiled roof where an enormous bougain-villea draped a thick crown of brilliant red flowers all year long. Unlike the expansive green lawns of Montgomery, all the houses on our new street were very close together with only a small sandy plot of land for a yard. The southern California air was cooled by the ocean, so house windows were always kept wide open, and at night you could lie in bed and listen to the waves crashing on the beach. Opposite the ocean and just a couple of blocks to the east of our house was Newport Harbor, where yachts and sailboats of every size and color bobbed on the dark-blue water.

After spending all our of lives in sleepy, staid Montgomery, my sisters and I were amazed to be in such a different and excit-ing place even though it meant we once again had to share a bedroom. The house was close to bursting for a family of six, not including our black cocker spaniel, Lady, and our cat, Sunshine.

Every weekday morning before dawn Daddy, Jane, and I would get in the car and make the forty-five minute drive to the sprawling campus of Autonetics. Because we were working on projects contracted by the military, we all had to have spe-cial clearances to get in, which made us feel very important. Jane worked in the ditto department; she would run huge rolls of paper through the giant ditto machines and be covered in ink by the end of the day. Thankfully my job as a file clerk was much less messy.

Weekends were spent exploring our strange, wonderful new world, from waving to the glamorous people cruising by on their yachts in Newport Harbor to browsing the motley array of shops near Balboa Pier, where you could buy a bikini in every color of the rainbow or eat a frozen banana dipped in chocolate. Determined to become real "California girls" right away, my sisters and I lay out in the sun until we were nut-brown and bleached our hair with peroxide, much to our mother's dismay. When the sun went down, Jane and I would steal away to join in the bonfires that groups of young people made on the beach, where we'd sneak sips of beer, smoke cigarettes, and sing along to the strains of a badly tuned ukulele.

The days of summer went by fast, and soon it was time to start thinking about returning to Auburn for my junior year. But despite Daddy's new job—one he was doing very well—there was not enough money to pay my tuition. He had sold the furniture store at a huge loss, and the debt collectors, who had followed us to California, even repossessed the family car one night while we slept. I would not be going back to Auburn for my junior year. If my parents worried that I'd be devastated by the news they didn't need to. Although I'd enjoyed my two years at Auburn, I also loved living in the new, modern world of southern California. It was a place where anything seemed possible, even for a naïve girl from Alabama.

When the news got back to Auburn that I would not be returning, two of the musicians from the Knights flew all the way out to California and pleaded with me to come back. "We have to have you, Toni!" they said as we sat in the small living room with the ocean breeze blowing through the curtains. "You're our singer . . . you're our *girl!*" I was touched by their insistence and amazed to realize just how much I'd been valued in the band. But the truth was I didn't want to go back to stodgy Alabama and be forced to walk around campus in skirts and pearls. My summer in Newport Beach had made me realize just how huge and exciting the world was. California was irresistible; its sparkle of opportunity was just as potent to me as the gleam of gold had once been to thousands of prospectors. Deep inside I knew there was something special there just waiting for me to find it. And in the dawn of the 1960s, if you were young and full of dreams, California was just simply the place to be.

CHAPTER 5

AFTER OUR FAMILY CAR WAS REPOSSESSED—A PAINFUL REMINDER that the family's debt had not completely been left behind in Alabama—Jane and I pooled our earnings and bought a car to share. We found a 1952 Ford Crown Victoria, pale pink with rusty edges, at a used-car lot and made weekly payments until its $300 price was satisfied. Then, with great pride, we christened our pink princess "Fannie Mae." Fannie Mae promptly thanked us for liberating her from the car lot by blowing out a tire on the drive home. Despite a shaky start, the car ended up being a much-needed and dependable mode of transportation not just for Jane, Daddy, and me to drive back and forth to Autonetics, but for the whole family.

On our free days, Jane and I would drive Fannie Mae about fifty miles away from sleepy Newport Beach to the bustling, glamorous enclave of Hollywood. It amazed both of us to be in that mythical place we had only known from movies and film magazines. We would walk up and down the sidewalks looking at the stars' handprints and marveling at the magnificent movie palaces like Grauman's Chinese Theater. These theaters were elaborately decorated—each more fantastical than the next—with mirrored ceilings, gold-leaf moldings, and red velvet curtains. We would watch a double feature at one theater and then run down the block to catch a movie in another theater. Occasionally we'd splurge on lunch in one of the fancy restaurants that lined Hollywood Boulevard, dining on lobster, shrimp salad, and other exotic delicacies. It was incredibly exciting, for two awestruck girls from Alabama, to be there in the heart of Hollywood, where it seemed everything wonderful happened. After having our fill of rich food, movies, and excitement, we'd climb back into Fannie Mae for the trip back to Newport Beach.

The little house on Balboa Peninsula was overflowing, and I was old enough to live independently from the family, so I decided to get a place of my own. I found a tiny apartment in an old house just a few minutes away on Balboa Island, a thumbprint of land nestled in the azure waters of Newport Bay. Mother gave me a few pieces of furniture, and I added my own "bohemian" touch by hanging some colorful macramé tapestries on the wall. There was much to love about my newfound independence, but in reality I was still just a "square" southern girl thrust into a fast-moving and unfamiliar world.

The free-spirited culture of southern California could not have been more different from the conservative South where I had been raised. I remember when some girls I'd become friends with invited me to go have a drink with them at a local hangout. When I asked in bewilderment how we could possibly go to a bar when we didn't have a man to go with us, they burst out laughing. I realized with great amazement and more than a little embarrassment that here in California women could go anyplace they wanted without a man and that *no one would think anything of it!* In Alabama a woman would never go to a bar without a male escort, or even out to dinner alone; it was absolutely unheard of. California was a place where the old rules were discarded, and I was a little intimidated by the brash and often reckless attitude that people my age possessed. But despite my traditional upbringing, I was determined to fit in, and I knew that I'd never go back to Alabama.

My parents and sisters were only a short ferry ride away, but I sometimes felt lonely in my little apartment. There was still tension within the family too. Mother, having been uprooted from her career and sense of structure back in Alabama, was unhappy in California. The family's abrupt departure from Montgomery created a whirl of gossip and mean-spirited speculation, a kind of schadenfreude that can often be expected from people when misfortune falls on the lives of others. Mother held her head high, but I know it bothered her knowing that many of the same people whom she'd once considered friends were now talking behind her back. Starting a new life in Newport Beach was more difficult for my mother than anyone else in the family. She didn't know anyone, and because we drove our only car to work every day, she was stuck in the house much of the time. Bored and frustrated, she began to put on a lot of weight. Daddy, while doing very well at his new job, still had his sporadic drinking binges. It was apparent to everyone that the move to California had not been the magic cure for my parents' unhappy marriage.

Like many young people who are suddenly thrust out into the big, scary world on their own, I saw the life ahead of me as mundane and lonely. Although I didn't dislike my job at Autonetics, it was hard to imagine being there my whole life, clocking in and out daily, and doing the same thing for years on end. *Surely,* I thought, *there had to be more to life than this.* I'd given up college, so there was no hope for any kind of job in teaching. Deep in my mind lurked thoughts of Daddy's thwarted dream of a singing career: *Was I destined for the same fate? Where was my place in the world? And would I ever find it?*

To alleviate my loneliness, I started pouring myself a glass of brandy when I came home from work. One glass eventually became two. The sweet, strong liquor relaxed my tense shoulders and helped take an edge off the boredom. *So this was why Daddy drank,* I realized with a faint tremor of alarm. Though I restricted myself to only two glasses per night, I was ashamed that I liked the way it made me feel. And I found that when the initial warmth of the alcohol had faded, I'd feel even lower than I had before. Depression, I now know, had run a dark thread through my family for generations, but it wasn't until my early twenties that I first experienced its manipulative power. There were even times when I wondered if life was worth living at all.

When the emptiness of the apartment became too much, I'd go out and walk around the harbor alone for hours. The island would often be dreamlike, cloaked in dense fog with the winking lights of boats anchored out in the bay and the mournful call of tugboats moving along the distant canals. I could see people through the lit windows of the homes along the water and hear their snatches of conversation or peals of laughter. Other people would be out on their own nocturnal strolls around the bay, in pairs or solitary like me. Every couple seemed to be so happy and in love. I wanted to be in love too. Whenever a young man went by, I couldn't help but glance at his face and think, *Could* he *be my soul mate?*

Sometimes Jane and I would go sit on the beach at the Wedge, a surfing spot off the Balboa Peninsula, famous for its enormous and often dangerous waves, to watch the surfers. Their bold defiance of death or injury just to ride those huge, bone-crushing walls of water was thrilling to witness. We would flirt with them a little bit, and the boys were always fascinated by our southern drawl. But I always felt very shy. The surfers, with their sun-browned skin and salt-bleached hair, were absolutely gorgeous to look at, but they were never my idea of the perfect boyfriend. The ideal man for me wouldn't be quite so simple, I decided. He would be complex and soulful and maybe a little bit dark. Little did I know at the time just how complicated the man I'd eventually fall in love with would be.

The boys I was interested in were more likely to be brooding over jazz music at one of the local cafes than surfing at the beach. One night I went out with some of my girlfriends to listen to a jazz group playing at a club. While the band was taking a break between sets, I struck up a conversation with the drummer, whose name was Ken. We began dating, and things quickly got serious, but deep inside I had doubts that Ken was the right person for me. We both loved music but, honestly, that was just about the only thing we really had in common. Ken had lived in California his whole life and had been brought up very differently than I had.

Jane graduated from high school and a year later, in 1961, married a dark-haired Marine fighter pilot named Bill after a brief courtship. In a small but lovely wedding thrown in full relief against a brilliant blue California sky, Jane wore the same satin wedding gown that Mother had worn when she married Daddy. As I stood by in my pale-blue organza maid of honor dress watching my younger sister leave with her dashing new husband, knowing that the very next day she would be moving to Hawaii where Bill was stationed, I felt a pang of anxiety. I was the oldest girl—shouldn't *I* have been the one walking down the aisle? Wasn't that what a good southern girl was *supposed* to want? And so, although I knew it wasn't the right decision, I married Ken the following year.

Why did I marry a man I didn't truly love? I think I married him because I felt lost and it seemed the logical thing to do. After our wedding, Ken enlisted in the army and we moved to Georgia, where he went through basic training. Once again I found myself back in the sleepy, red-dirt landscape of the South. We lived in a small, off-base complex built for married couples, a grim place with peeling linoleum and roaches scuttling behind the pasteboard cabinets. There wasn't much for me to do except clean the apartment and drink coffee with the other wives, most of whom were just as bored as I was. Children yelled and threw sticks at each other in the dusty, chain-link-fenced yard. The radio was my best friend during the many hours I spent alone, and I sang along with the hits of the day by Neil Sedaka and Brenda Lee. Sometimes I found myself drumming my fingers on the table as though it was a piano.

Ken drew a meager salary from the army, but money was so tight that our idea of a party was when we provided the Kool-Aid mix and our guests brought the sugar. Mother sent me letters with news of home and would occasionally fold a twenty-dollar bill in the pages. My eyes would fill with tears at the sight of the money, not only because I was horribly homesick but also because we were so broke that any amount meant so much. And I knew that it was difficult for Mother to send even a small amount since money was also tight for my parents, who were still providing for my two younger sisters.

If my marriage had been happy, money problems might not have mattered as much. But my relationship with Ken, which had never been strong from the start, began to unravel. His mild-mannered personality hid a temper that could flare into a frightening intensity. Ken never hit me, but once he got so angry that he threw his expensive camera on the floor, dashing it to pieces. *Who is this man I'm married to?* I thought in dismay, my hands trembling as I picked the pieces up off the ground. I didn't know the answer. It was an unsettling moment that I have never forgotten.

It was a relief when Ken was sent to Japan after he finished basic training and I could flee back to California. I resumed work at Autonetics as a security receptionist in the Research and Development center, checking in high-clearance visitors to the department: top scientists, engineers, and military brass. My work uniform was a slim-fitting suit, like something a chic flight attendant would wear, and shiny black pumps. I thought I looked very glamorous, and I must have because I received many compliments from the men who came to the center. I was flattered by the attention, but I also worried. After all, I was now a respectable married woman, and I shouldn't be getting winks from strange men! The solution, I decided, was to dye my blond hair dark brown. And what do you know; it worked! Once I became a brunette, I actually did notice a decline in admiring glances. Eventually I went back to blond hair, since that is what I felt most comfortable with, and sure enough, the men started to flirt again. But I was always faithful to Ken, despite his long absence from our increasingly estranged marriage.

Ken had always believed that the two of us could have some musical success as a Las Vegas–style lounge act. When he was discharged from the army and got back home to California, we went out on the road as a music group, with Ken on drums, me on vocals, and a friend of Ken's on keyboards. Our small group played gigs all over the country, which sounds really exciting but was anything *but*. We drove from state to state, in one car with all our instruments and luggage crammed in the back, and per-formed at hotel lounges and small clubs. The worst part for me was the cigarette smoke that billowed as thick as Newport Bay fog in every place we played. Thus began my lifelong dread of smoke because of its horrible effect on my voice.

The cigarette smoke was bad enough, but often the audience was inattentive and seemed completely uninterested in who was onstage. Sometimes we'd have a great, appreciative crowd, but many of the gigs were, quite frankly, a disaster. I'll never forget a freezing-cold night in Fargo, North Dakota, where we were dismayed to find we'd been booked at a country music club. No one had thought that maybe a Vegas-style lounge act wouldn't be such a great fit for this rough crowd. The audience was foul-tempered and drinking heavily, and their anger toward us grew the more they drank. They kept shouting for us to play "Wolver-ton Mountain," a popular song of the day that we didn't know. After a quick set, we hastily packed up and ran out the back door before the bottles started to fly!

We landed in Detroit for a few months where, in the mid-1960s, a lot of great music was happening—but not from us. After one gig that Ken had lined up for us fell through, I managed to get a job singing at the Caucus Club, a celebrated music venue on the bottom floor of the Penobscot Building in downtown Detroit. The Caucus Club had the look of an old gentlemen's club with dark wood paneling, leather banquettes, and brass railings. It had a wonderful house accompanist named Matt Michaels who helped me work up a selection of cabaret-style songs for an act. In exchange for singing, I made $150 a week and could eat for free at the club's London Chop House restaurant. Now that was quite a perk for a girl who had previously subsisted on canned soup and bologna sandwiches! Because Ken wasn't able to find work, we were both living off my meager earnings during our stay in Detroit.

Shortly before I got the gig at the Caucus Club, another singer had been in residence there. She was described as a striking young woman who dressed in a very bohemian-style in a potpourri of thrift store clothes. The people at the club said she had been unpredictable and eccentric, but she had the most spectacular voice and with it a steely determination to succeed. She did become a huge star shortly after leaving Detroit. Her name was Barbra Streisand.

In an attempt to supplement my wages from the Caucus Club, I tried to get work doing radio commercials. There was one audition where I sang a jingle for a milk commercial. I thought it had gone well, but the agency called and told me that I had been passed over for it because I sounded too "black." My first thought was, *Don't black people drink milk too?* But I also thought it was a wonderful compliment because most of my favorite singers were black! Later, when Captain and Tennille began to be played on the radio, we were one of the few white acts to be aired on the soul stations. Nothing could have pleased me more.

With Ken unable to find work and fed up with the bitterly cold weather, we finally headed back to California and tried to make a life together there. But we had drifted so far apart that we seemed to be living on totally separate planets. Needing some kind of creative outlet—and an excuse to be away from the house—I began to act in community theater plays. One time Mother and I were cast as the mother and daughter characters in the play *Picnic.* We were onstage in front of a packed audience doing a scene, and I realized that Mother had forgotten her line! She stared at me blankly as I scrambled to figure out a way that I could seamlessly cue her without the audience knowing. Somehow we got through the scene, and it was something we laughed about for a long time. Later I joined the South Coast Repertory

Theater, which is now a Tony-award-winning regional theater housed in a large, beautiful building but was then just a small community venue run out of a storefront on a shoestring budget.

By now Ken and I had separated and we would eventually divorce in 1972. I was working at Autonetics again and spending all my free time doing theater. A friend who was a director at the South Coast Repertory theater, Ron Thronson, told me he was writing a musical. It was about ecology, a theme that was rapidly gaining interest in the late '60s. He needed someone to write music for the songs and asked me if I might be interested in taking a shot. I had only written a couple of songs in my life, just for fun, but I agreed to try. He gave me the lyrics, I wrote the music, and we both really loved the results. Together we created a musical revue called *Mother Earth* that we opened at the South Coast Repertory Theater in 1969. On opening night *Hollywood Reporter*, *The LA Times*, *Variety*, and the *Orange County Register* all came to review it. To our delight all four papers gave the show fantastic reviews. After word got around about *Mother Earth*, Hollywood producers began to come down from Los Angeles to check it out. One producer, Ray Golden, an older guy who'd had some success in vaudeville-type productions, took us aside and said he could take *Mother Earth* all the way to Broadway! He quickly offered a contract, and we signed it, convinced we were on our way to the big time. We should have known better.

I was about to learn the first and hardest lesson I would ever learn about the cruel reality of show business. What we had done without realizing it was sign over all artistic control of *Mother Earth* to Ray Golden, who immediately insisted on changes that horrified Ron and me. He wanted the show to be "sexier" and demanded that the girls in the chorus wear hot pants, which completely diverged from the original vision Ron and I had for the production. Anytime we objected, Mr. Golden would remind us that *he*—not we—now had contractual control of the show! We stood by helpless and heartbroken while the beautiful story we had created together was chipped away and altered beyond repair. It went from a lovely, uplifting story about protecting the earth to a raunchy spectacle that none of the cast felt good about. Still, because we had naïvely signed that contract without understanding it, we were obligated to run the show for the dates that had been booked.

While we were playing our first professional showing of *Mother Earth* in San Francisco, at the Marines' Memorial Theater, our keyboard player announced that he was unable to join us for the later shows in Los Angeles. I needed to find a replacement, so when a friend recommended a keyboardist who was on break from his tour with the Beach Boys, I immediately set up a meeting.

The keyboardist had been given a recording of me singing songs from the show and liked it, so he agreed to fly up from LA to audition. I first saw him in the lobby of the theater, a rail-thin, pale young man with large brown eyes and scruffy dark hair. He was dressed all in black and slumped on a bench, arms crossed in an aloof, bored manner. But when he sat down and began to play, I immediately knew he was perfect for the show. And there was something about him I found intriguing. His long, slender fingers would play the music perfectly note by note, and then suddenly switch to an entirely different tune right in the middle, improvising for a few bars before going back to the first song. It was like he was telling me jokes through the music, and it made me laugh. When he finished and looked up at where I stood next to him, our eyes met. I felt my heart tighten and pound like a fist beneath my breast. We had our new keyboard player, and his name was Daryl Dragon.

CHAPTER 6

DARYL DRAGON WAS TWENTY-NINE WHEN I MET HIM IN 1971 and had already established a reputation as a promising young musician on the professional circuit. Like me, music was in his DNA and he carried an impressive pedigree on both his father's and mother's side. His father, the composer and arranger Carmen Dragon, was a true maestro, darkly handsome with a presence strong and magnetic enough to captivate an audience all the way to the very back row. Carmen wrote music for many films and television programs; he had won an Academy Award in 1944 for his part in the musical scoring of the Rita Hayworth movie, *Cover Girl*. He was also famous for his heart-pounding, original score for the 1956 movie *Invasion of the Body Snatchers*. Eventually Carmen became a founder and the lead composer for the Hollywood Bowl, and he conducted the Glendale Symphony Orchestra. He also produced a large number of pop-classical albums, including a rousing arrangement of "America The Beautiful." Carmen's arrangement was wildly popular when it debuted, and it continues to be the most commonly performed version of the song for July Fourth celebrations and presidential inaugurations.

Daryl's mother, Eloise, a delicate woman with translucent white skin and a halo of dark hair, had been a well-known singer in her younger years. She possessed an ethereal true coloratura soprano voice that could hit notes so high that the sound was preternatural. Often her soaring, angelic vocals were heard in movie scenes in which a religious experience was taking place. Eloise's voice made an eerie cameo in the terrifying climactic scene of the *Invasion of the Body Snatchers* film, which was scored by her husband.

Talented, successful, and socially prominent among the Hollywood scene, the Dragons raised their large family of three boys

53

and two girls in a beautiful Spanish-style home overlooking the Pacific Ocean in Malibu. But despite its glossy exterior, I would soon find out that the Dragon family life had been far from perfect; in reality it was quite disastrous to the emotional health of Daryl and his siblings.

When Daryl arrived in San Francisco to audition for *Mother Earth*, he was on a break from backing the Beach Boys as a keyboardist. Later, he told me that it was only when he listened to the recordings of me singing some of the songs I'd written for *Mother Earth* that he'd really become interested in working with me. We were busy wrapping up the last dates of *Mother Earth* in San Francisco, but within those weeks of nonstop rehearsals followed by two shows a day in Los Angeles, I felt myself more and more intrigued with the enigmatic young man who said little but watched me with his large, liquid-brown eyes. The quieter he was, the more I was determined to draw him out. I didn't know it at the time, but this kind of hide-and and-seek dance would become the choreography of our long-term relationship.

Two people could not have been more different. With my long surfer-girl blonde hair and ample zaftig curves—nourished by late dinners of San Francisco's famous Reuben sandwiches and cookies from the catering table backstage—my presence had the intensity of a loose bolt of electricity bouncing from wall to wall. Even if I felt shy in a particular situation, I could always summon the courage to act as though I were the most confident person in the room—a trait that became invaluable when facing large audiences and television cameras.

In contrast, Daryl never felt obligated to put on any other face than the one he was feeling at any given moment. This "shyness" later became his signature style; he was the impassive man behind the keyboards with the beautiful brown eyes and virtually no voice at all. I was left to fill in the awkward, empty gaps Daryl left with happy words and laughter, a duet that lasted nearly the entire time we were together.

I immediately hired Daryl as our keyboardist, and he finished out the last *Mother Earth* shows with us in Los Angeles. I was relieved to finally be done with the production, which had become such a disappointment thanks to Ray Golden, but the arrival of Daryl in my life seemed like a silver lining. I would find myself watching him as he played, his head bobbing to the beat as his fingers flew over the keys. Offstage I engaged him with talk about music for the show, which was the only way I could really get a conversation started. I was fascinated with him, but Daryl never gave any hint that he was interested in me other than as a musician. Never one to give up, I kept trying to figure him out.

We began to spend time together, going to see live music or eating out at the health food restaurants he frequented around Los Angeles. I quickly learned that Daryl was a strict vegetarian and adhered to a rigid, macrobiotic diet. Today, health food can be delicious, but back then it was just plain *awful*. Our dinners out were mainly brown rice and steamed vegetables, with so little seasoning they were practically tasteless, but I gamely ate them anyway because I wanted Daryl to like me. One benefit of this Spartan diet was that I lost quite a few of my deli-sandwich pounds. Meals with Daryl might have been "healthy," but they were never particularly tasty—or joyful.

Although Daryl didn't share many details about his private life, I gradually began to piece together a little bit about him. He told me that he'd recently had a troubled girlfriend, Carol, who was a well-known groupie around Los Angeles. She had been a true "party girl" who at one point had consorted with Jim Morrison and other famous rock stars. Carol would disappear for days, traveling with the hard-partying entourage of some big rock bands. The manic life as a groupie wore down Carol, who was emotionally fragile and prone to addiction. She would call Daryl, crying and begging him to come pick her up.

Shortly before Daryl and I met, Carol, who had developed a serious drug habit, had hit rock bottom with tragic consequences.

After driving up to a secluded part of the Malibu hills, she'd washed down a bunch of sleeping pills with a bottle of liquor. Her body wasn't discovered until three days later.

Daryl showed little emotion when he told me this story—he seemed most fixated on the belief that someone had slipped her LSD, and that was what had pushed her over the edge—but I was sure he was just keeping his pain concealed. How could a person not be affected by something so terrible? I felt so sorry for him that I just wanted to sweep him up in my arms. I also began to wonder if I was the kind of girl that Daryl would ever be interested in. The groupie girlfriend had been petite, dark, and wild—while I was this Amazonian blonde in long paisley skirts, dependable down to the minute, who didn't do drugs and only drank occasionally. In retrospect the contrast probably made me even more determined to "win" Daryl over and prove that I too was interesting and worthy of his love and attention—and that I was the woman who could "save" him from all the heartache that he'd experienced in the past.

He didn't make it easy for me. Most of the guys I'd met who were interested in me would make their intentions well known, but Daryl never did. Our shared interest was always music, and when *Mother Earth* was over, we spent a lot of time listening to records and discussing different styles and techniques. I knew he respected me for my talent and loved my voice, and though I was already infatuated with him, I couldn't tell if he was attracted to me in the romantic sense.

One time, I went to the beach with him and one of his friends, a loud and flirtatious guy who made no secret that he admired how I looked in my bathing suit. I tried to laugh it off and be polite, but it made me very uncomfortable. The whole time Daryl watched with a cryptic little smile. I realized later that he was probably "testing" me to see how I would react if another man tried to get my attention. The previous girlfriend had never been able to resist other men, which perhaps had hurt him more than he cared to admit. But I was not that kind of girl at all and was determined to prove to Daryl that I wanted *him* only! The Beach Boys were about to start touring, and Daryl, who would again be joining them on the keyboards, told me that they were looking for an acoustic piano player to substitute for their regular pianist who was taking a year off. Then he added that he thought I would be perfect for the job and asked if I was interested. "Well, of course I'm interested!" I exclaimed. "Who *wouldn't* want to play with the Beach Boys?" By that time they were one of the biggest bands in the world and well into establishing their musical legacy with a string of infectious, rhythm-infused hits like "Little Surfer Girl," "Help Me Rhonda" and "California Girls." It was the opportunity of a lifetime, I thought, and a chance to spend some time with Daryl. Maybe being on the road would help to deepen our bond. "But don't I need to audition first?" I asked. "They've never heard me play!" Daryl assured me that he'd already vouched for my playing ability with Carl Wilson, the band's singer and musical director. I would "try out" before the first show of the tour, which kicked off in Binghamton, New York. All I had to do was pack a bag, fly there with Daryl in a couple of weeks, and pray that the Beach Boys would like me.

After two whirlwind weeks of learning all of the Beach Boys' music, Daryl and I met the band and their crew at the airport to fly to New York. I sat in the airplane gazing out the window with the soaring music of Gustav Holst's *The Planets* playing through my headphones. As we flew east, the clouds parted behind us to reveal a glorious sunset. Pink, violet, and gold melted together, dissolving into misty blue around the edges that deepened toward the heavens, where a single star winked like a diamond pressed into indigo velvet. I glanced over at Daryl, who sat dozing off next to me, and felt an overwhelming wish that he could feel a little bit of what I was feeling. Instead I turned back to the window and watched as the sun dipped below the horizon and slowly bled its color from the sky, until all I could see was the vast expanse of space that was now speckled with stars. *Who was this man next to me?* I thought. *What kind of role will he have in my future?* An inner voice whispered to me that fate had brought us together and something very special was going to happen.

The whirlwind of rock-and-roll touring life began the moment we touched the ground in New York. We were whisked to the venue for rehearsal inside a vast, echoing place with tour managers shouting orders and roadies rumbling by as they pushed stacks of amplifiers on carts. Outside, the fans had already begun to gather, pushing on the locked doors and peering in through the glass. Up on the stage Daryl pointed to a piano, and I sat down obediently. The other members of the band slowly emerged one by one, picking up their instruments to start the rehearsal.

That little girl who had trembled years ago in Miss Gill's hallway, waiting for her piano recital to start, now sat on a stage about to play with some of the biggest rock stars in the world. Daryl and I had already worked together creating lead sheets for some of the Beach Boys' songs so they could be copyrighted, since the two of us had the ability to translate music by ear into notes and chord changes on the page, but this was different. I took some deep breaths and looked over at Daryl, who gave a curt nod of encouragement from behind his keyboards. Carl held his hand up to signal the first song, "Wouldn't It Be Nice," and on the count, we began to play. I kept my eyes on the music, reading the notes while listening to the blend of the other instruments around me. After a few moments, I noticed Carl sidling up to stand beside me while he sang. He was watching me play! My heart pounded along with the driving rhythm of the song, and I tried to keep focused. What if he didn't like me? I would be so humiliated, for myself and for Daryl who had vouched for me. After a few agonizing seconds, Carl turned and drifted away. I glanced over at Daryl and he smiled with a little shrug of his shoulder. I'd passed the audition.

It was an unbelievable experience for me to be involved with this enormous production, where the screaming audiences stretched row after row all the way to the back of the auditorium. I quickly learned some painful lessons about playing live with a rock band. On one of the first nights of the tour, we were playing in Philadelphia, and the crew set up a stack of guitar monitors right behind my piano. During the entire concert, all I could hear was the deafening, shrill screaming of the guitars. When I got offstage, my ears were ringing, and for days afterward I felt as though I were under water. When I mentioned it to Daryl, he looked at me like I was an idiot and said, "Well, why didn't you wear earplugs?" Daryl had neglected to mention that I might want to wear earplugs, even though as an experienced touring musician he always did. But it had never occurred to him to warn me.

Being the only girl in a band full of men posed other challenges. The Beach Boys had a rabid following of female fans who pressed their bodies along the front row of the stage and tried every trick in the book to get backstage. At the start of the tour the security guys would stop me when I was trying to get onstage before a show, thinking that I was a groupie who had managed to slip in. "No," I'd patiently explain, "I'm in the band. Yes, *really*." There had never been a girl in the Beach Boys, so they thought I was lying. After that, the tour manager made a point of introducing me to the security team in each new venue, letting them know that, yes, I really was in the band and therefore I was "legit!"

Any worries I had about being accepted into an all-male band were quickly set aside once the guys realized I could play. The only person who didn't receive the new "Beach Girl" as warmly as the others was the middle of the Wilson brothers, Dennis. It took me a while to figure out why he obviously disliked my presence when everyone else was so welcoming. Dennis was incredibly talented and wrote several of the wonderful songs that the Beach Boys recorded. But it was his older brother, Brian Wilson, who was considered the real genius of the group. By the time I joined the tour, Brian, who hated the stress of touring and was dealing with emotional issues, had quit the road. The more reclusive

Brian became, the more his legendary status grew, eclipsing his younger brother's.

Like Brian, Dennis also had an incredible ability to sit down and improvise a beautiful song, but he didn't have the musical training to put the notes on paper. So Daryl would work with him for hours, listening to Dennis play the songs over and over and writing down the notes and chords. In a way, Daryl was the conduit for Dennis's music, and I think Dennis came to depend on him. Perhaps the fact that both Dennis and Daryl were raised by mercurial, overbearing fathers created some kind of intuitive understanding between the two of them, although I doubt they ever talked about it. When I entered the picture, I believe Dennis saw me as an unwelcome distraction for Daryl's attention.

One day during the tour, Daryl and I were riding in a car Dennis was driving. Dennis seemed moody and withdrawn, as he often became when I was around. He began to drive faster and faster, running through stop signs and taking curves erratically, all the while staring straight ahead. I hunched in the backseat, terrified, gripping the side of the car while it swerved in and out of traffic. We managed to reach our destination without having an accident, but I couldn't help but feel that some of Dennis's vitriol was aimed at me. Later, I would get similar treatment from Daryl's brothers, who saw me as a barrier to their own musical aspirations.

I hoped that Daryl and I were going to become closer while on tour, but it didn't happen quite as I'd imagined. For one thing I realized just how strict Daryl was about food; even the limitation of meal choices on the road didn't stop him from adhering to his stringent diet. He solved this problem by bringing his own food supplies—including a hot plate and a pot—packed in an old metal ammunition case. While the rest of the crew ate at local restaurants or ordered in pizzas and sandwiches, Daryl would set up the hot plate in his hotel room and cook brown rice or bulgur wheat. Then he'd mix in a few tomatoes or onions, and that was what we'd eat—*every single night*. I was ravenously hungry the entire tour, but wanting to please Daryl, I dutifully ate what he served without objection.

Sometimes Mike Love would join us in Daryl's hotel room and eat whatever health mush Daryl had prepared. At that time Mike was deep into his spiritual period with the Maharishi Mahesh Yogi, the creator of the Transcendental Meditation technique and personal guru to many famous bands, including the Beatles. Mike spent a lot of his free time meditating or talking about the metaphysical philosophy that "His Holiness," as devotees of the guru referred to him, taught. Before the band went onstage, Mike would gather everyone around to repeat spiritual mantras together. Some other members of the band were also followers of the Maharishi, and their brand of incense-choked piousness sharply contrasted with the behavior of those in the group who were still indulging in the full-on rock-star life of drinking, drugs, and groupies.

Once when we were all in an airport, some people from our group sat down lotus-style on the floor to meditate, chanting as they did so, while people walked around them on the way to their gates. To many of the people walking by we must have looked like a bunch of lunatics! I thought the whole thing was kind of weird, but I've always felt that people should do whatever makes them happy. And being on the road with a group as fabulous as the Beach Boys was a huge thrill. Although I'd been hired just to play acoustic piano, occasionally they'd ask me to chime in on the backing vocals. It was a hectic but exciting time. It was also the first time I saw firsthand how far some fans would go to gain access to their idols, something that would affect me later in my own career.

Some kind of ambiguous relationship had developed between Daryl and me while we traveled on the tour, but he still refused to say, or show, anything about his feelings toward me—if he *had* any feelings toward me at all. Daryl was like a locked door with only little slivers of light shining around the edges that made me increasingly determined to get in. But there was something else in his eyes when he watched me sing that was almost as good: admiration, and maybe even pride. I knew that Daryl recognized my talent and love for my craft. He realized that, together, we had a special chemistry. What he did share with me was not a declaration of love or the whisper of sweet words in my ear or even a warm embrace.

But for the time being, I would take it.

CHAPTER 7

Back at home in Los Angeles, in between tours with the Beach Boys, Daryl and I began to spend more time playing music together. He possessed impeccable, classically trained skills and an inexhaustible drive for perfection that both intimidated and inspired me. It was wonderful to find someone who took the creation of music as seriously as I did and who encouraged me to write my own songs. Daryl's interest in being my musical partner pushed me to try harder. I wasn't particularly ambitious, but music, I'd come to realize, was one of the few ways that I could attract Daryl's attention.

Over the course of a year we'd slowly become romantically involved. But being romantically involved with Daryl was not what most people would consider romantic. We didn't hold hands. He would never kiss me unless I initiated it. When I tried to hug him, his embrace was tentative, as though he was uncomfortable with the closeness and couldn't wait to be released.

At the time I figured there was some kind of wall that had yet to be breached in Daryl's psyche. It was, I believed, just a matter of patience and willpower before the wall would finally yield, its stones having been gently loosened one at a time through the sheer persistence of my love. Many years later when I became an avid fan of the television show *The Big Bang Theory*, I was amazed at the similarities in the awkward "love" story between two of the characters, Sheldon and Amy, and the way Daryl and I had been. Sheldon, a genius theoretical physicist, is all facts and emotionless practicality, while his more adoring and romantic girlfriend Amy, a microbiologist, is always trying to break through to him and turn him into the loving man she dreams he can be—without success. On *The Big Bang Theory* this tug-of-war romantic struggle between Sheldon and Amy is a delightfully comedic plotline, but in real life it is heartbreaking.

In those early days, I was embarking on a journey of faith that Daryl would start to love me the way I loved him. The love and desire that I wasn't confident enough to communicate to him were instead channeled into songwriting—for that was how I felt safe enough to let him really know my feelings. I might not actually be able say it, but I sure could sing it.

All we needed now for our fledgling musical duo act was a good name. After toying around with some pretty awful options we decided on "Captain and Tennille." Mike Love had given Daryl the name of "Captain" while he was on the Beach Boys tour, in homage to the driving boogie piano solos Daryl would pound out on songs like "Help Me Rhonda" and "Fun, Fun, Fun." At that point Daryl had already taken to wearing a captain's style hat that he'd found in a military surplus store.

"Ladies and gentlemen," Mike would say when Daryl was about to break into one of his piano solos. "Here he is, Daryl Dragon, the captain of the keyboards!" We both liked the unique ring that my family name had, so we combined the two and became "Captain and Tennille."

We hired an agent to help us secure some gigs around town, and with her help we got booked for a three week run at the Apple Valley Inn, a hotel and restaurant outside of LA owned by the cowboy star Roy Rogers. His stunt horse Trigger, who had passed away by that time, had been stuffed in a rearing position and was displayed in a large glass case where tourists could pose for pictures. The Apple Valley Inn had been popular for decades as a vacation destination for celebrities and music industry executives, so being there meant some possible good exposure and, just as important, a steady paycheck.

Daryl decided that this would be the perfect time for the two of us to go on the "grapefruit diet" that he had heard about. This meant we couldn't eat anything except white grapefruit—they had to be the white ones, not the pink or red ones, which were sweeter—for three weeks. When I asked him what the point of such a draconian diet was, he declared that it would "fix" our damaged genes, thus preventing both physical and mental disease. Huge bags of grapefruits slumped on the floor of our hotel room, filling the air with their sour, acidic scent. I began to grow weaker and weaker each passing day, barely gathering up enough energy to perform at night. My clothes hung from my body, and cheekbones I didn't know I had emerged on my face. Daryl, who was already skinny, grew positively gaunt, but the thrill of this fanatical self-torture seemed to empower him. At that point in our relationship, I was still holding my tongue about Daryl's crazy ideas, so I did exactly as he proposed and ate nothing but grapefruit the entire time we were at the Apple Valley Inn. Well, *almost* the entire time.

Things finally came to a head during the last week of the diet. One of the activities at the Inn was horseback riding, which I had loved since I was a girl at summer camp. But halfway through what should have been a pleasant trail ride, I could hardly keep myself upright on the horse. My head ached terribly, and the landscape seemed to swim before my eyes. I thought I was going to faint and had to grip my saddle horn just to stay on my mount. When the ride ended, I staggered off my horse and made my way to the kitchen where the staff was preparing lunch. The first thing I saw was a bowl of rolls, and I grabbed one, shoving it into my mouth right there in the kitchen. Then I ate another, and another. I probably looked like someone who, covered with dirt and half-crazed from starvation, had just wandered in from the desert, but I didn't care. As long as Daryl could not find out, I'd content myself with sneaking real food and not push the issue.

Back in our hotel room, the trashcans were spilling over with the damp, curling peels of all the grapefruits we consumed every day. The housekeepers must have thought we were off our rockers. Of course, in retrospect I look back and think, *What an idiot . . . I should have thrown the damn grapefruit on the floor, gotten up, and gone down to enjoy the lavish dinner buffet with everyone else!* But I didn't. I believed that this diet was another kind of "test" that Daryl was subjecting me to, and I was determined to pass it. If I didn't, I was afraid that he would see me as weak and flawed.

On the day we left the Apple Valley Inn, it was finally time to break the magic grapefruit fast. Daryl said the only safe way to ease back into solid food was to eat popcorn, so before leaving we fixed up a huge bag of it and put it between the seats of the car. All the way back to Los Angeles we munched on the popcorn. After three weeks of *starving,* the salty taste of warm, crunchy carbohydrates in my mouth almost brought tears to my eyes. I tried to eat the popcorn slowly while also sipping on a lot of water, but Daryl kept plunging his hand in the bag and eating large amounts. By the time we got home, I was starting to feel normal again, but Daryl suffered an unexpected consequence of all that roughage on his empty stomach: He was horribly constipated for days! I may have lost some weight, but after all that trouble I doubt that any of our genes were healed by the miserable grapefruit diet.

Except for the three-week gig at the Apple Valley Inn, Daryl and I both knew that going out on a "motel lounge" tour around the country, as I'd done with my first husband, was not a smart career move. We were exactly where we needed to be: Los Angeles, the center of the music industry universe at the time. It was where the people who made things happen in entertainment lived and played. When we first started looking for gigs around town, Daryl took over the role of cold-calling the clubs. He'd ring one up and when someone answered he'd say, in a monotone voice, "Umm, hello . . . I'm a duo looking for work." It made me cringe just to listen. Clearly, Daryl's musical charisma did not carry over to his telephone skills, and we didn't land any jobs. I was way too shy to call by myself, so we recruited one of Daryl's friends who possessed a strong, confident voice and gregarious personality to make the calls on our behalf. Thankfully it worked, and as a result so did we.

Once we got started, the work came more frequently. We had hired a Hollywood agent, a sweet blonde lady named Dolly, to help us secure some gigs. With Dolly's help we began to play several times a week at places around Los Angeles, bringing in a regular, if still modest, income. The clubs we played ranged from large to small, each with its own unique microcosm of patrons. There were many wonderful nights at a gay bar called David's, where the rapt audience swooned in appreciation when we played the really dramatic, romantic songs like Carole King's "(You Make Me Feel Like) A Natural Woman." David's, with its well-mannered and enthusiastic crowd, was always a pleasure to play.

Other venues were not. Ron Perranoski's Stadium Club, owned by the famed LA Dodger pitcher, had a permanent odor of stale beer and grease topped by a thick fog of cigarette smoke. The smell nearly knocked me on my back the first time I walked in. We played there maybe twice, but the smoke became too much for me and I refused to go back. Another gig we had for a while, at O'Shaughnessy's Irish Pub in downtown Los Angeles, was better . . . until St. Patrick's Day came around.

Daryl and I had been booked there for a couple of weeks, playing our usual routine of ballads and pop songs to what was typically a friendly and receptive audience. But on St. Patrick's Day, the crowd at O'Shaughnessy's became something entirely different. The place was packed with people wearing green paper hats and drinking vats of green-tinted beer, and they were there to celebrate St. Patrick's Day as loudly—and drunkenly—as they could. Daryl and I sat down to play, but after a few songs the crowd started to yell out for us to play "Irish" music. The only Irish song we knew was "O Danny Boy," so we played it as the audience happily sang along. When we resumed playing our regular songs, the crowd became agitated and called for more Irish music. Their inebriation increased as the night went on, and the "requests" began to sound more like angry demands. So, Daryl and I started in with another round of "O Danny Boy" and the crowd, momentarily placated, burst into a cheer of delight. In order to appease the audience we probably played "O Danny Boy" more than six times that night. But honestly, they were all so drunk I doubt they realized that we were repeating the same song!

When we got booked at the Smokehouse, a venerated music club and restaurant in the San Fernando Valley, things began to look up. The Smokehouse was known as the place to hear up-and-coming musical acts and as a result, drew a bustling and glamorous crowd, with actors, television and movie people, and record executives making regular visits. On the downside, the Smokehouse, like most of the other places we played, lived up to its name: it was *extremely* smoky. This was the early 1970s and it seemed that *everyone* smoked—which posed a lot of problems for my voice. We'd go on at 9 p.m. and play four sets until well after midnight, with brief breaks in between. In between sets I'd run outside and gulp in the fresh air, trying to clear my head and vocal cords before going back inside. The experience was often so anxious for me that I wrote a song about it called "The Good Songs":

> Lord, I just can't make it tonight,
> Too many things just didn't go right.
> And I just can't get that glow on,
> I just don't think I can go on tonight . . .
> But then I feel the lights in my eyes and endless faces
> looking at me,
> and I hear them cry, "Make us happy tonight,
> Bring us music, give us light!"
> And I just start singing . . . and the love comes tumbling out . . .

The Smokehouse became a regular gig for Daryl and me throughout 1972 and 1973, and we began to build a local following of fans. I remember arriving at the club for gigs and being astonished to see that people had begun to line up outside before our set even started! We played many of the pop hits of the day by Carole King, Elton John, and Billy Joel while sprinkling some of our own original music in the mix. Always wanting to please the crowd, we gladly took requests, but there were two very popular songs that I refused to play because I just didn't like them very much. Helen Reddy's "I Am Woman" was one, and Tony Orlando and Dawn's "Tie a Yellow Ribbon Round the Old Oak Tree" was the other. People loved those songs and sometimes would offer us large tips to play them, but we never did. If they persisted, I'd tell them that the band at the club down the street would play them. I doubt that the owners of the Smokehouse would have been very happy if they had known that I was sending Smokehouse patrons to another club!

Some of our friends from the Beach Boys crowd would come out to the Smokehouse to hear us play. Bruce Johnston, an extremely talented songwriter who had been a part of the Beach Boys for years, came in one night. After our set he told us that while he thought we were pretty good, a record label would *never* sign us because we were too old! I was just thirty-two years old at the time and Daryl was thirty. Adding insult to injury, Bruce also scoffed at the name of our duo. "Nobody will ever be able to pronounce or spell the name 'Tennille,'" he snorted. Thankfully, we didn't take Bruce's opinions on either subject to heart.

It wasn't just smoke that could be hazardous when we played the clubs. Except at the Smokehouse, Daryl and I were still responsible for getting all of our own equipment into the venues where we played. Daryl needed all of his keyboards and I my electric piano, and these instruments weighed a ton. I swear it's a miracle that I didn't break my back while Daryl and I lugged them from the car through narrow club corridors and up onto the stage. Then when the gig was over, we'd have to break everything down and carry it all back out again. I thought to myself, as I staggered backward down the stairs under the weight of Daryl's four-hundred-pound Hammond B-3 organ, that if I ever "made it" in the music business the first thing I'd do would be to hire a roadie to haul the gear!

"Disney Girls," a beautiful song written by Bruce Johnston that we covered in our act, had become a favorite with our Smoke-house audience. One night a local DJ told us that if we recorded "Disney Girls," he'd play it on the radio. We were thrilled at the idea of having one of our songs played on the radio, so we scraped some money together and went to a small demo studio to record a 45 rpm single. We needed a song for the flip side of the record and decided on "The Way I Want to Touch You," a song I'd writ-ten one night in a New Jersey hotel while we were on tour with the Beach Boys. The song had been floating around in my head for days, and I was just dying to sit down and write it. But to do so required a piano. I went down to the lobby one night and asked the guy behind the desk if there was a piano anyplace in the hotel. He thought for a moment and then remembered there was an old piano down in one of the ballrooms. "But it probably is out of tune," he added. It was, but I didn't care. Alone in the empty ball-room, I sat down and poured out all of the physical and emotional longing I had to "touch" Daryl with my love.

I had never done a professional recording before, and the pro-cess proved quite stressful for me. I often burst into tears because Daryl, who could not tolerate error, at times became impatient and critical. I was responsible for both the lead vocals and the backing vocals, which Daryl would record on separate tracks and then layer over the song. But somehow we got through it and successfully made a record. We pressed about three hundred of the 45s on our own label, which we named "Butterscotch Castle" after the tiny stone cottage that Daryl and I were living in at the time. Then we dropped it off at the radio station where the DJ had said he would play it.

After that, with our brand-new records under our arms, we took to the streets, plodding around town from radio station to radio station to ask the DJs if they would play it. Once we went through all the stations around LA, we hit the road in our VW bus. Along with our new bulldog puppy, Broderick, we traveled all over the West promoting the record. I think we covered over four thousand miles in about three weeks! All we had for a travel guide at the time was a paper road map, and since most of the radio stations were located outside of town, we'd end up driving around for hours looking for them.

In those days a radio station was ruled over by a music director, who pretty much decided what would and wouldn't be played on the air. The music director would have to like not just the song, but its promoters too! Since Daryl wasn't the greatest communicator, it was usually up to me to talk the music director into giving our record a listen. And boy, that's where the southern charm that had been drilled into my head since childhood really paid off: I knew how to make a real connection with people. Fortunately, most of the music directors seemed to like the record. When the last of the 45s had been given out, we headed back home to our Butterscotch Castle, broke and utterly exhausted, and waited to see what would happen.

To our surprise it wasn't "Disney Girls," which was so beloved in the clubs, that became a listener favorite; according to the radio stations, it was the B-side song, "The Way I Want to Touch You," that people were calling in to request the most. A local distributor pressed some more copies to put in Wallich's Music City, a huge and famous record store in Hollywood on the corner of Sunset and Vine. When it quickly went to the top-ten on Wallich's sales charts, they called to ask us if we had more records to bring in, because they were sold out! It was apparent that we were on to something.

Although Daryl had the most talent and skill, his two brothers, Doug and Dennis, were also musicians. Before I entered the picture, the three had put together a rock group called The Dragons; they had played a few gigs around town but didn't really go anywhere. Where Daryl was disciplined and focused, his brothers appeared, to me at least, erratic and volatile. When Daryl and I met and began to spend more time playing together, he gradually lost interest in The Dragons. And when we created Captain and Tennille, he quit the band completely—much to his brothers' chagrin. Daryl, with his tough work ethic and music expertise, had been the driving force in the group. Without him to keep things together, Doug and Dennis would have little chance of success on their own. As Captain and Tennille began to get noticed, I could sense their growing contempt for me. Similar to the situation involving Dennis Wilson, here I was again standing in the way of someone else's personal access to Daryl. Doug in particular seemed to aggressively dislike me. I came to dread being around either of them and tried to keep my distance.

But I didn't have much time to worry about the Dragon brothers. Things were starting to happen with Captain and Tennille, starting with "The Way I Want to Touch You" making it to the top of the local radio charts.

CHAPTER 8

WHILE "THE WAY I WANT TO TOUCH YOU" WAS RISING UP THE charts, Daryl and I kept our regular gig playing at the Smokehouse. The crowds got bigger as people from outside the city who had heard our song on the radio began to come see us play. The record company people in the audience were paying more careful attention to this peculiar new duo calling themselves "Captain and Tennille." Between our sets we were led around to shake hands with people from RCA, Capitol Records, and some of the other big labels in town. Soon after, the offers began coming in. Daryl and I found ourselves faced with more options than we'd ever dreamed of, but before either of us signed *anything*, we were determined to maintain creative control of our own music. I had not forgotten the painful experience of losing control over the musical *Mother Earth* and was hell-bent never to repeat it.

After signing a new act, a record label would typically assign a staff producer to work with the artists on their first albums. The producer had a lot of power over the direction and sound of an album, which could be either good or very, very bad, and the latter is something that Daryl and I were not about to risk. We both knew that Daryl was the only person who could produce Captain and Tennille so that the music kept the unique personality we'd worked so hard to develop. But because we were new artists, most of the major record labels that we'd talked with balked at giving us this kind of freedom. As a result we turned down every single offer until A&M stepped forward.

By the time they came knocking on our door, A&M Records was the largest independent record label in the world. Started in the early '60s by the famed trumpeter and bandleader Herb Alpert and his friend, music entrepreneur Jerry Moss, the label had become a formidable presence among the larger, corporate-run record companies. Herb and Jerry shared the rare philosophy that new artists should be allowed a certain amount of creative independence and room to grow, unlike the other labels that were quick to drop an act if sales of their first record did not produce a hit single. A&M had taken the same unorthodox approach in 1969 with The Carpenters, who had become one of their top-selling acts. A&M agreed to our stipulation that Daryl and I would produce our first album for the label, and if it did well, we'd be allowed to continue recording without a staff producer.

The day we signed the contract was a blur. I remember us crowding into the A&M conference room surrounded by Jerry Moss and Herb Alpert, a gaggle of label executives and pro-motion people, and our various managers—whom we'd quickly enlisted to help us out. Champagne was popped, and so many photos were taken that my face ached from smiling. It may sound cliché, but that day I really did feel that at any moment I'd wake up to find that it had all been a dream. I kept looking over at Daryl, thinking back to when we first met and were on an air-plane flying off to play with the Beach Boys, which was when I first sensed that something special was going to happen between us. And here we were. The contract signing was very exciting, but Daryl and I couldn't wait for the party to end so we could head straight into the studio to start work on our album.

First though, we had to decide which songs we would include on our first record. We decided on five original songs that I had written, two by Bruce Johnston, and two Beach Boys covers. One of those songs, "Cuddle Up," had been co-written by Den-nis Wilson and Daryl. We started recording these right away. In the meantime Kip Cohen, head of A&M's Artists and Reper-tory (A&R), started searching for other songs that would suit our style. Kip was one of the finest A&R men in the country. He knew his artists, studied their styles, and had a natural talent for knowing what songs would work best with each. Kip worked tirelessly with Daryl and me. He listened to countless song demos and studied proposals from music publishing companies looking for just the right songs to suggest to us. After we had recorded all the songs we had chosen, we realized that something was missing from the album. We needed a catchy, up-tempo song to liven up the succession of ballads.

One day Kip called us into his office to hear an album he thought might have some potential—a record Neil Sedaka had released in the UK titled *Sedaka Is Back*. All the songs were great, but one stood out from the moment we heard the first few chords. It was called "Love Will Keep Us Together" and was exactly the sound we needed. A&M agreed, and because the charts were very ballad-heavy at that particular time, they felt that an upbeat song would do well. We went into the studio the very next day to record it.

Recording "Love Will Keep Us Together" was one of the best experiences of my life. While Daryl played most of the instruments and I played acoustic piano on the tracks, we finally had the luxury of hiring some of the best studio musicians available to accompany us. Most thrilling of all was to have the drummer/percussionist Hal Blaine, who had been part of the legendary group of studio musicians who were known as the "Wrecking Crew," working on the album with us. He was, and still is, considered one of the most prolific drummers in recorded-music history, having played with everyone from Elvis Presley and Brian Wilson to Steely Dan. An extremely likeable and enthusiastic fellow, Hal had an innate sense of rhythm and knew just how to make a song sound its best. It was an honor to have him in the studio with us.

We were like kids in a candy store; we had the most up-to-date recording equipment and instruments right there at our disposal and a spacious studio to work in that was so comfortable we rarely left while we were making the album. In the past when we performed in clubs and it was just Daryl and me playing, I'd had to play the piano with my right hand while playing the bass on the Moog synthesizer with my left—in addition to singing! It was wonderful to be free to concentrate on just singing or just playing the piano.

For backing vocals I happily enlisted all three of my sisters; each had her own distinct, lovely voice. Melissa, who was classically trained in opera, lent her soaring lyric soprano vocals, hitting those high notes the rest of us couldn't. Louisa's voice had a distinctive "kid-like" quality that Daryl and I both loved. Jane had initially flown out from her home in Nashville just to watch the recording but ended up lending her sweet soprano to Bruce Johnston's "I Write The Songs." Melissa's husband, Andy Boettner, now a renowned southern California vocal teacher, sang tenor. Even Mother sang a few notes on one of the songs, making the album a true family affair and one I'll never forget creating.

While we were recording "Love Will Keep Us Together," I playfully added "Sedaka is back" to the sing-along refrain of "Dah ... dah dah dah dah" as the song faded out in a medley of applause and whistles. Initially we thought this would be cut out of the final version, but once we played it back we realized it was actually a great way to end the song. And it was also our homage to Neil's album, where we'd first heard the song.

A&M's impressive headquarters were housed in Charlie Chaplin's former studio near Sunset Boulevard in Hollywood, a sprawling campus of offices and studios intersected by open-air courtyards. While walking through the halls it was possible to cross paths with Cat Stevens, Peter Frampton, or other top artists who were also with A&M or just recording there (A&M had one of the best recording studios in town). While we were making our album I became acquainted with the studio's hit brother-and-sister duo The Carpenters. Richard Carpenter was a kind of recording savant who could spend hours going over the same song until he felt that it was perfect. He had his own reserved parking space at the front of the studio and his *impossibly* shiny black Mercedes Benz sports car would be parked there for what seemed like days at a time. Karen, whose beautiful, cello-like voice I deeply admired, always seemed to be running to keep up with their grueling work and touring schedule. She was sweet but very reserved, with large brown eyes and a shy smile hiding what would later be revealed as a deep and ultimately tragic inner turmoil.

One time I was in the ladies' room washing my hands when Joni Mitchell walked in and crossed behind me to enter one of the stalls. Joni was a true legend, and I had always been in awe of her amazing talent and the poetry of her lyrics . . . and there she was in the same ladies room! Just like any star-struck fan, I dawdled at the sink waiting for her to come out, my heart pounding with excitement. When she came out and stood next to me at the sink our eyes met briefly in the mirror. I was still a complete unknown and even if she had known who I was, Joni possessed the kind of effortless cool that made me feel like the girl who comes to the party in a dress when everyone else is in jeans. Not knowing what to say, I just smiled and nodded before racing out the door. Even after Captain and Tennille became famous, I never felt comfortable around many of the rock artists of the day who all seemed to be members of some hip society that I was too "square" to be part of.

A&M hired the famous rock photographer Norman Seeff to take our picture for the album cover. We went to Norman's house for the shoot, a very California-bohemian place where, it seemed to me, an awful lot of hippie-looking people were hanging out. I also remember Norman's lovely young wife nursing a child that looked to be at least three years old. It wasn't her lack of shyness that surprised me the most, but the fact that she was breastfeeding a child old enough to eat a hamburger!

Norman had won a couple of Grammys for his work and possessed a true genius for capturing the spirit of his subjects through the camera lens. He immediately hit on the idea to have Daryl and me pose, casually dressed, against a white background with our bulldogs Broderick and Elizabeth. In the photo Daryl is dressed in his signature black turtleneck and round dark glasses, his lips pressed into a kind of half-smile. Meanwhile I, with a huge toothy grin and my hair cut into what would become my signature "Toni Tennille" style, have one arm around Daryl and the other around Broderick.

It was, everyone agreed, the perfect picture of a quirky, happy couple simply having *fun*—the very symbol of optimistic, modern romance that Americans in the mid-'70s, beleaguered by the Vietnam War, rising divorce rates, and inflation, were desperate for. The funny thing was that when that album was made, Daryl and I were not yet married. But that didn't seem to matter. In 1974 women's liberation and sexual independence had become the rally cry of a new generation, and the shame of "living in sin" seemed as outdated as college girls wearing long skirts and pearls—except, I must add, for my conservative southern mother who was always uncomfortable with the idea that Daryl and I were living together without being married.

The album *Love Will Keep Us Together* launched in November of 1974. The title song immediately hit the charts and began to climb higher as the weeks went by. I remember when I first heard it on KHJ—the biggest top-40 radio station in Los Angeles—while driving down Ventura Boulevard. When I heard my own voice coming through the speakers, I nearly drove the car off the road. I was so excited that I had to pull over into a service station to compose myself! Friends and family began calling from all over the country, saying that our songs were in regular rotation on the radio in their towns. Someone else who heard us was Howie Greenfield, the famed songwriter who had written the lyrics to "Love Will Keep Us Together" with Neil Sedaka. When he first heard it on the radio, he immediately called up A&M. "Who is that doing "Love Will Keep Us Together?" he asked. "It's just fantastic!" A&M told him it was a new act they had recently signed called Captain and Tennille. Howie said he wanted to meet us. "Are they black?" he wanted to know.

Howie and Neil had started out in New York, working together for the publishing company Aldon Music in the art deco Brill Building, famous for its elaborate, brass-clad façade. There they joined a team of other writers churning out entire catalogues of American hit songs for Connie Francis, The Shirelles, Bobby Darin, and other top performers of the time, which helped to make Aldon one of the most lucrative music publishing companies in the world. Neil's success as a performer took off in the mid-'60s with top hits such as "Breaking Up Is Hard to Do" and "Calendar Girl," just two of the many songs he wrote with Howie. Nearly a decade later Neil and Howie would collaborate again on "Love Will Keep Us Together," which, as I recounted, Neil recorded and released in England.

We both loved Howie immediately; he was a warm, gracious man, welcoming us into the beautiful Beverly Hills home that he shared with his long-time partner Tory Damon. Eventually Daryl and I would become regular guests at Howie and Tory's home where they hosted wonderful dinners and gatherings for small groups of friends who, for all their varied successes in the entertainment industry, were generally down-to-earth people. At a time when the music industry was becoming known for fostering a raucous, druggy, party atmosphere, Daryl and I always felt relaxed and at ease with Howie and his friends. We also got to know Neil, who became a good friend and a longtime supporter of our music. I have never seen anyone who loved to perform for an audience more than Neil Sedaka. The sheer joy he projected as he sang and played his wonderful songs was absolutely infectious, and I couldn't help but smile when I was around him.

By the summer of 1975, "Love Will Keep Us Together" had hit number one on the *Billboard* Hot 100 list. Suddenly we were not just all over the radio waves, but were also being invited to perform on television shows like *The Merv Griffin Show, The Midnight Special, Dinah!* (Dinah Shore), and *The Tonight Show*. Our advisors began administering every aspect of our image, making suggestions on everything from what kind of outfit I should wear to how Daryl and I should stand together when we were in front of the press. While Daryl could get away with donning his usual black suit and hat, my look was carefully scrutinized by the publicity people. They felt that I needed to look glamorous without losing any of my "girl next door" affability, so many long discussions ensued about which dress I should wear when appearing on television. I was to look sexy enough to be interesting but not enough to shock the audience! The single phone in our house went from ringing just occasionally to practically being shaken off the walls with constant calls from our managers and agents, informing us of requests for publicity appearances, interviews, and meetings.

We began to receive so much fan mail at A&M that one of our advisors recommended hiring someone to oversee our fan club. Fan club? Daryl and I had been so busy we hadn't even thought of such a thing, but all of a sudden it was important. We enlisted a married couple who had been fans from our early days at the Smokehouse, and the two went to work opening and sorting letters and sending our personal responses along with autographed photographs. Daryl and I were both blown away by the wonderful things fans wrote about how much they loved our songs and the personal stories they shared. This outpouring of love and appreciation touched me deeply, because I'd never dreamed that so many people would ever listen to our music. I was determined that every fan who wrote was responded to.

Very quickly, we started being recognized when we went out in public. The sudden fame was exciting, but it also made me nervous. I thought it was a bit scary. I began to realize that our private life was suddenly very interesting to other people, and I wasn't ready to discuss it because I wasn't sure *myself* what was going on between Daryl and me. Of course, I was still full of hope that Daryl really did love me but was just unable to express it yet, for some reason. I knew people thought we were perfect "lovebirds," but that was not true. I found at that point that I had to begin what would be a decades-long attempt to keep the reality of our relationship to myself.

Although attitudes toward marriage were changing in the mid-'70s, the entertainment industry still kept a rather self-consciously prudish stance on how their artists' personal lives were viewed by the public. The very essence of what Captain and Tennille stood for was devoted romantic love, and in those days that generally meant *married* romantic love. When our album came out, Daryl and I were still living together—*sans* matrimony—in our little rented Butterscotch Castle. Flustered and worried about negative press, A&M decided to issue a press release announcing that Captain and Tennille had been married on Valentine's Day 1975. They neglected to say anything to us about it, however, so it wasn't until fans began mentioning it in their letters that we learned our record label had "married" us. "You got married on Valentine's Day?" one letter gushed. "That's so cute!" Other fans sent in pillows festooned with pink and red hearts and our "wedding date" needlepointed on them. We were furious at the publicity people for their little prank, but by then it was too late. I had no choice but to go along with the story, although lying to our fans made me feel incredibly guilty.

The wedding rumor only fueled my mother's zeal to see us legalized. "But Toni," she'd often say in a slightly reproachful southern lilt. "Daryl's from such a *fine* family. You're already living together, so I can't understand why you two aren't married yet!" To Mother, the fact that Daryl was from such a glamorous and successful family only underscored the perfection of our union. She had no clue about just how dysfunctional the dazzling Dragon family truly was. From the start, she'd been bewitched by Daryl's handsome father, the famous conductor, and his angel-voiced mother, who lived like two characters out of a Hollywood fairy tale in their oceanside home in Malibu. I had already gleaned from Daryl some of the abuse that he and his siblings had suffered at the hands of their father. Here was another talented family much like ours had been: gilded on the outside but deeply flawed within.

But thanks to the Valentine's Day press release, everyone now thought we were married, so it seemed only logical that we actually should go through with it. In fact, now that we were making a lot of money, our accountant had been encouraging it because of the tax advantages married couples had. Daryl didn't actually propose; when we decided to marry, it was as though we were picking out what color paint to use in our new house. In retrospect, I believe that he approached the issue with the same emotionless rationality that he applied to any of the other many business decisions we were making. What should have been one of the happiest moments of my life—and a comforting validation of what I hoped was Daryl's true, if unspoken, love for me—was almost an afterthought.

CHAPTER 9

OUR REAL WEDDING TOOK PLACE IN THE FALL OF 1975. WE HAD decided to get married in Nevada because it was quick, and we figured that no one would recognize us. Even though we had a number-one hit record, we hadn't been on television that much at the time, so we thought we could get the deed done "under the radar." Las Vegas was the obvious choice for most people wanting a quick and easy wedding, but I hated the thought of getting married in such a flamboyant and crowded place. So we flew up to Reno, Nevada. But once we got there even Reno, while smaller than Las Vegas, still didn't seem quite right. After consulting a map, we decided on the remote hamlet of Virginia City about an hour's drive away, and we took our vows inside a tiny chapel tucked into the Silver Queen Saloon.

A former silver mining town, Virginia City retained much of its "Wild West" charm even almost a century past its glory days. There was still snow on the ground as we wound our way up the mountain to the dusty, sleepy little town that from a distance looked like a village from a toy train set. What we didn't realize was that the day we had selected to get married—November 11—was Veterans Day, and all government offices were closed! Undeterred, we made our way to the courthouse where we found a lone clerk working overtime in the office. After learning how far we'd come, this kind lady took pity on us and went ahead and issued us a marriage license. When we asked about a justice of the peace who could perform the marriage ceremony, the clerk thought for a moment and then said that we might be able to find him in one of saloons on Main Street.

After walking in and out of the many saloons, we finally located the Justice of the Peace sitting at the bar with his hand cupped around a glass of whiskey. Fortunately he was an amiable old fellow, and probably two or three deep into his afternoon libations. So despite the day being an official holiday, he agreed to perform the ceremony. He instructed us to go down the road to the Silver Queen Saloon, which had a small wedding chapel, and he'd meet us there once he'd finished his drink. When he arrived, we realized that we didn't have any witnesses, and according to Nevada law we needed two. Once again the Justice came to our rescue by enlisting a guy dressed in old-time western garb with a garter on his arm who was playing honky-tonk piano in the saloon bar. Then he found another man who was eating a sandwich at the saloon's lunch counter, and we had our two witnesses. Within five minutes the deed was done, and the Justice told us we'd receive our marriage certificate in the mail.

When we walked out of the dark saloon into the bright November sunlight, I wondered if the whole thing was real. There hadn't been any wedding photographer to document the occasion, but we came across a photography shop where tourists dressed up in western gear and saloon dresses to pose for old-time souvenir pictures. There we changed out of our dusty jeans into the costumes we'd each selected: a high-necked lace dress and large feathered hat for me and a sheriff getup for Daryl complete with a badge and a rifle. There we stood for our one and only wedding photograph.

After our somewhat odd but entirely legal wedding, I didn't feel any closer to my new husband than I had before. I wonder how many other new brides—even those who'd had a much more traditional ceremony than I—felt the same way as they waited for the romantic fairy tale, which had been promised to us since girlhood, to start. Daryl and I had stood in front of the Justice of the Peace and two unknown witnesses, all three of questionable sobriety, in a tiny chapel inside a darkened saloon that smelled of smoke, whiskey, and beer, and pledged our love and devotion to one another. Though the sentiment was achingly real on my part, I had doubts that it was on his. But there was still time, I told myself. Surely once the hectic pace and distraction of our lives slowed a bit, we could settle down and concentrate on what mattered most: each other.

But there were other things to be happy about. The executives at A&M and our publicity team breathed a collective sigh of relief that Captain and Tennille could finally live up to the wholesome, untainted image that made us so beloved to our fans. Mother, while disappointed that we'd chosen to elope instead of having a proper wedding, could not have been more thrilled that Daryl and I were *finally* married. And we had managed to get hitched without any press hearing about it, leaving most of our fans to continue to believe we'd been married on that sweetest of dates, Valentine's Day.

Another major change happened following the months that *Love Will Keep Us Together* hit. For the first time in my adult life, I didn't have to worry about money. When we got our first check from A&M, I just stood there staring at it in disbelief. I had never seen such a large amount of money written on a check—and it was ours! Although there wasn't much time to go shopping, everyone agreed that the first thing we needed to do was buy a new home befitting our freshly minted star status. So we said good-bye to our little Butterscotch Castle and bought a house in Pacific Palisades.

Keeping it in the family as I always tried to do, I had enlisted Mother, by then a licensed California real-estate agent, to find us the house. She found a beautiful 1930s home in the exclusive enclave in the leafy hills between the Pacific Ocean and the Santa Monica Mountains. Originally built for film director Joseph Mankiewicz, the house was French-country style, with a gabled roof and an ivy-covered stone façade.

After renting for so many years, I was excited to finally have a chance to decorate my own home—and boy, did I ever go to town! Whenever I could take a break from our busy schedule, Mother and I would scour the décor shops and auctions looking for just the right pieces. Money was now no obstacle, but I still leaned more toward a comfortable elegance instead of Hollywood glitz, because I felt a home should be a place for relaxing and not for showing off. I did go a little crazy with wallpaper and ended up using a different color and style in every room! There was the "yellow" room, the "peach" room, the "blue" room, and so on; the décor might have seemed a little too motley for some people, but it suited me just fine.

Daryl and I had always had separate bedrooms from the time we became a couple. People were often surprised to learn that even as newlyweds, we preferred sleeping apart. But after spending so much time together in the studio or on the road, we both needed some personal space at the end of the day. Also, I have always been a reader and Daryl usually wanted to listen to the radio well into the early hours of the morning, so having our own rooms allowed us to relax in the ways we each liked. In our new house I claimed the largest bedroom for myself, which had a little fireplace with hand-painted French tiles and wide oak floors. Going for the full-on romantic look, I put up dramatic floral wallpaper of pale peach begonias on a black background, billowing sheer lace curtains on the windows, and a pile of plushy pillows on the bed. It was the perfect place to curl up on a chilly night with my dogs and, when he felt like it, Daryl, and read a book while the flames crackled in the fireplace. There wasn't much time to do that, though, because usually when I got home after a busy day I'd fall right to sleep!

The fan mail kept coming at a steady pace, much of it wanting to know about our personal lives. Fans asked us about our dogs, how Daryl and I had met, and what we ate. They also would send in various items, such as record sleeves, posters, or magazines, and request that we autograph them. But most of the questions were about Daryl. They wanted to know why he was named "The Captain" and why he always wore a hat. They wanted to know why the Captain never smiled. Did he even talk? It was clear that Daryl's enigmatic persona was having quite an effect on our fans, and they wanted to know more about him. Little did they know how much I shared that sentiment.

People were also curious about when and if we would have children. At that point in time, Daryl and I were both so busy that having children was the last thing we were thinking about, but in all honesty, neither one of us had ever voiced much of a desire to have any. I was thirty-five years old by the time we married and did not see any way that I could raise children and keep up my hectic career. Besides, I was very concerned about the mental illness that was present from far back in Daryl's family history. The Tennilles had some skeletons too, but they were mostly addiction issues; I wasn't aware of any serious mental-illness genes like those that the Dragons had.

But we didn't come out and say any of that, of course. Instead, we turned the attention over to our two bulldogs, Broderick and Elizabeth, who really *were* our children! The dogs went everywhere with us and became just as much a symbol of Captain and Tennille as my haircut or Daryl's hat. We even took them with us when we were guest performers on talk shows such as *The Tonight Show*, where they promptly upstaged Daryl and me with their unaffected charm and lolling tongues.

Thinking back, perhaps I was using the dogs as a kind of distraction from the lingering isolation that I felt in my relationship with Daryl. It seemed that everyone wanted to believe that we had a "perfect" relationship—romantically and professionally. And although it remained unspoken, there was no hiding the fact that A&M believed that our appeal as a couple sold records as much as our music did. The appearance of a crack in that shining image could have an adverse effect on our careers. Even more important than that to me, though, was keeping up the assumption that Daryl and I were truly, deeply in love.

The 1970s had heralded new attitudes toward sex, drugs, and hedonism, much of which was reflected in the music being produced. It was an interesting time because so many different styles and sounds were emerging all at once. For example, the Doobie Brothers with their whiskey-tinged rock and roll shared the charts with Frankie Valli's string-heavy ballad "My Eyes Adored You." The pop earnestness of the late '60s was still there, but a darker, moodier sound was starting to surface from the Eagles with their soaring California-style rock and Linda Ronstadt's smoky, sexy cool. Disco, freshly imported from the kinetic dance floors of New York gay bars, was just starting to bubble up in new releases from the BeeGees and Diana Ross.

Artists like The Carpenters and, of course, Captain and Tennille, occupied a space somewhere in between, layering a soulful classicism over a steady pop foundation. The musical variety available over the airwaves allowed people to find their own means of self-expression. America, as a nation, was in the process of discovering its own kind of cultural independence, which was underscored when we celebrated our bicentennial in 1976. And no place embraced the right to personal expression, individual freedom, and decadence as much as Los Angeles.

Now that we were a hit, Daryl and I were often invited to record industry parties and events. Here, among the fast, glamorous set, guests would sometimes do cocaine as casually as sip a cocktail. Daryl, with his steadfast adherence to only "healthy" things, never drank, and neither of us smoked or used drugs. But many other people in the industry who were flush with money, prestige and a tendency toward self-destruction, indulged to great excess.

I remember being at a party in a gorgeous Beverly Hills mansion that was reportedly owned by Diana Ross—although if it was, I never saw her when I was there. All the beautiful, cool people were there—actors, models, musicians, record industry people—dressed in the latest designer clothes and looking impossibly chic as they smoked cigarettes and sipped wine. As the party progressed, I noticed that people kept going in and out of a closed door down one of the hallways. While looking for the restroom, I wandered down the hallway just as the door to the room opened. Inside people were sitting at a table around a large mirror covered with lines of white powder. A man was bent over the mirror holding a straw. He looked up and smiled, beckoning me to come in the room. I shook my head and quickly walked away leaving an eruption of laughter behind me.

After that incident, no one ever mentioned drugs to me or Daryl again. We both had our reasons for abstaining: I had seen the devastation that alcohol addiction had done to my own family, and Daryl had dealt with his two brothers, one of whom had his own alcohol problems when they had been in a band together. The squeaky clean image that stayed with us all the years we performed as Captain and Tennille made us sort of outsiders in the social side of the music business. Since we didn't "party," it was assumed we could not have been any fun to be around.

But the truth was that even though Daryl and I were not part of the wild scene, we were not "square" at all. If other people did drugs or drank a lot, then fine; it just wasn't the thing for me. I never wanted to be out in la-la land when I took the stage. It was important for me to always know where my "base" was so that *I*, not the drugs or alcohol, was in control of my performance. Daryl and I were both dedicated to making music, and we treated it like the full-time job it was. After a full day of recording, appearing on television shows, or meeting with the label reps, I just wanted to crawl into bed with my dogs and fall asleep.

Of course, we knew that some of the people around us were regularly using drugs—from label execs to fellow musicians to studio technicians. In reality, Daryl and I were probably part of a very small minority who didn't use them. I couldn't help but notice the jittery hand gestures, extreme mood swings, and pronounced "sniffing" by certain people we worked with during meetings. It wasn't as though I looked down on those people, because some of them were great at their jobs and worked hard to help us become successful. But I never did understand the appeal that cocaine, pills, or marijuana had to so many of our peers. When we began to tour with a full band and crew, I was always kept blissfully unaware of what went on behind the scenes. As long as everyone did their job and showed up on time, what they did in their free time was their own business.

The pinnacle celebration for the music industry has always been and still is the Grammy Awards. The 18th Annual Grammy Awards, recognizing artists' accomplishments in 1975, was held in February 1976 at the Hollywood Palladium and broadcast live over national television. "Love Will Keep Us Together" had been nominated for Record of the Year, so Daryl and I were among the guests that streamed into the Palladium's glittering walkway, stopping on the red carpet to pose for photographs or chat with reporters. I'd brought all three of my sisters—Jane, Louisa, and Melissa—who had been so instrumental in providing backup vocals for the record. I wore a long sheer gown of daffodil yellow covered with shimmering beads and sequins with a matching choker. It was the first gown I had ever had designed just for me. Daryl looked more handsome than he ever had in a sleek tuxedo, black captain's hat, and ever-present dark glasses. Other artists attending the awards that night were Paul Simon, Linda Ronstadt, Glen Campbell, Barry Manilow, and members of the Eagles, who were also nominated for Record of the Year. Neither Daryl nor I thought we had a chance at winning the award, but just being there was an honor.

When the moment came to announce the winner of Record of the Year, I prepared to smile and clap graciously when the camera panned over us after we didn't win. Stevie Wonder took the podium to announce the winner, opened the envelope, and ran his fingers over the braille imprinted inside. Then with a great big smile, he leaned to the microphone. "And the winner is . . . *Captain and Tennille!*" For a moment we were both frozen in our seats as the audience burst into applause all around us. I looked at Daryl and saw that he was stunned too. As though in a dream, we rose and walked up the aisle to the stage toward an enthusiastically grinning and clapping Stevie. However, the folk singer Joan Baez—who was standing with Stevie at the podium—was *not* wearing a smile as she handed the Grammy to us. There was no doubting her obvious disapproval of a "hokey" pop couple like Captain and Tennille winning Record of the Year! The ungracious reception stung—but just for a second. Once I turned to the microphone, I completely forgot about it. On behalf of both Daryl and me, I thanked our fans, A&M, Neil Sedaka, and Howie Greenfield. I knew that my mother and three sisters sitting in the audience, and my father watching from home on television—all the people who had loved and believed in me since I was a little girl so small that my feet wouldn't touch the piano pedals—were sharing in my proud moment.

"Love Will Keep Us Together" had been named Record of the Year for 1975. We couldn't believe it, and neither, apparently, could our record label. For in the chaos after the event, as we shook hands and received congratulations and posed for pictures with our award, someone from A&M nervously approached to inform us that we were the guests of honor at the A&M Grammy party being held later that night. Guests of honor? We didn't even know that A&M was throwing a party! It finally dawned on us that until we won the Grammy, we hadn't actually been invited to our own label's party.

It was a prime example of our how our squeaky-clean image had kept us isolated from much of the entertainment industry social scene. The Grammy was the biggest event of the year and the after-parties, which often lasted until dawn, ran freely and quite openly with champagne and cocaine alike. The A&M party would be no exception. But because the Captain and Tennille had unexpectedly won one of the top awards of the night, hasty arrangements were made to get us to the party. Daryl and I made an appearance to a barrage of applause and cheers, shook some hands, and went home with our Grammy, leaving the rest of the party to celebrate as outrageously as they wanted.

So home we went, exhausted from the evening's events, and placed our shiny gold Grammy on a shelf in the living room over one of the grand pianos. I shook off the fancy dress that seemed to have become heavier as the hours had gone by and changed into my comfortable pajamas. Daryl disappeared to his bedroom, leaving me with the dogs snuggled on either side of me on the sofa. I looked around the room, filled with beautiful furniture and art that just under a year ago I'd never imagined that I'd be able to buy. How far we'd come in such a short amount of time! Here I was a newly married woman with a hit record and a Grammy, living the dream that so many artists aim for. A sudden pang hit me, a memory from long ago. At that moment I could easily still have been the girl who sat alone in her tiny apartment on Balboa Island, wondering when, and if, the loneliness would ever end. The man whom I'd thought was my soul mate was in many ways just as remote as a stranger passing by through the fog.

CHAPTER 10

"Love Will Keep Us Together" would eventually become the number-one record on the 1975 Billboard Top 100; it was often referred to as the "song of the summer." It was everywhere, blaring out from transistor radios at the beach and drifting from the open windows of passing cars. I was thrilled when I pulled up at a stoplight next to another car and heard "Love Will Keep Us Together" playing while the driver sang along.

At that time A&M had many artists on their label who were quite popular in Spanish-speaking countries, so they suggested that we record our entire first album in Spanish to see how it would do in those markets. I was able to speak a little bit of Spanish, and I thought the project sounded like a lot of fun. A&M found a lyricist who translated the lyrics into Spanish and also hired a Spanish language coach to help me get the pronunciation correct. The album *Love Will Keep Us Together*, or *Por Amor Viviremos*, became a hit in Mexico and many other Spanish-speaking countries. Years later after my song "Do That to Me One More Time" became a number-one hit in English, we released it in Spanish as "Amame Una Vez Mas." I thought, once again, that Spanish truly is the language of sensual love . . . that song really sizzles when it is sung in Spanish!

I think every artist who has had a huge success—whether it is music, a film, or a book—experiences the same kind of apprehension: What will follow next? After the initial flush of that first achievement has subsided, you start wondering if you'll be able to re-create the same kind of magic again. We had our fans, our record label, and our peers in the music world watching to see what we'd do next, which was both exhilarating and incredibly stressful.

There was no question that A&M wanted us to start recording a new album quickly, so we started making plans to head back into the studio to record our second album, *Song of Joy*. Daryl and I both thrived on the energetic, collaborative process of recording, and we were eager to get back into the studio. For the song list we chose another penned by Neil Sedaka called "Lonely Night (Angel Face)" and a beautiful ballad, "Thank You Baby," written by Bruce Johnston, our old Beach Boys colleague who'd written "Disney Girls." We also included one of my own songs, "Butterscotch Castle," which was really a children's song about the little rental house Daryl and I had once lived in. At that time I wrote for the pure joy of it, never worrying about whether the lyrics were "hip" or not, and "Butterscotch Castle" was a perfect example of the romantic, sentimental songs I loved.

It was a delight to find out later on how much children related to that song. My sister Louisa became a third grade teacher after she decided to retire from being a backup vocalist for Captain and Tennille. She was a wonderful teacher and her kids adored her creative approach to learning that included bringing lots of music into her classroom. "Butterscotch Castle" was one of the songs she liked to play for the students.

Louisa's classes were very mixed in race and financial circumstances, and many of her students lived on the edge of poverty. One day after she had played the song "Butterscotch Castle," she asked the children to imagine and draw their own picture of a Butterscotch Castle. When she sent the drawings to Daryl and me I was incredibly moved. Most of the drawings were of a colorful, happy house with a "big old dog" in the front yard and the "old gray cat" on the back porch, as the song lyrics go, and bold yellow rays of sunlight beaming down over tufts of bright green grass. But the thing that touched me so was that most of those kids did not live in a Butterscotch Castle. Some didn't even have a house of their own; instead, they lived with their families in motels or with foster parents. But still, they knew what the real Butterscotch Castle looked like in their hearts.

We included another song I had written on *Song of Joy*, "The 1954 Boogie Blues." I'd written it about Daryl's great love of the "boogie" piano style and his idolization of the players of that genre: Jerry Lee Lewis, Fats Domino, and Little Richard. When we performed that song in concert, audiences got a huge kick out of Daryl's rocking the piano during his boogie solo. He seemed to lose himself in the music, shedding all inhibition and even playing the piano with his feet and with his back turned to it as Little Richard and Jerry Lee had done! Daryl was in a rare moment of abandon and seemed to feel genuinely happy. Watching him play was like getting a rare glimpse of sunlight through a thick stand of trees and wishing that more of it would break through. I always hoped that his joyful mood would last beyond the song, but it rarely did.

Captain and Tennille were fortunate to have two hit singles from the *Song of Joy* album, "Lonely Night (Angel Face)" and "Shop Around," which was a cover of Smoky Robinson's great song, except this time sung from a *woman's* point of view. If an album produced two hit singles, as *Song of Joy* did, A&M would usually not release another single from that album. But that changed when they got a call from a radio DJ at WISM in Madison, Wisconsin, about the barrage of calls they had been receiving to play one of the songs on the album called "Muskrat Love." That DJ flat out told the A&R guy that if the label didn't release "Muskrat Love" as a single, they would be making a big mistake! A&M wisely took his words to heart and the song became the third hit release from the album.

Oh, "Muskrat Love!" It was only on a whim—a joke, really—that we had included that quirky little tune on our second album. It was a song that the audiences had loved when we'd performed it back in our nightclub days at the Smokehouse, and we reasoned that if it had been so popular there, it might also be a hit on the radio.

Originally recorded by the band America in 1974, "Muskrat Love" had been penned by the legendary Texas roots-rock songwriter Willis Alan Ramsey about two besotted muskrats named Sam and Susie. I'd first heard it on the radio as Daryl and I were driving to the Smokehouse for one of our performances and was intrigued by the wryly humorous lyrics. They made me laugh out loud! Although I had never seen a muskrat in my life, I could just imagine these two little cartoon-like furry creatures rolling together in the grass. Daryl, who was always game for anything "strange," liked it too and added in a melody of trilling, warbling "muskrat" noises with his synthesizers. The Smokehouse audiences had requested it so often that we had to make a rule that we'd only play it twice each night! When we decided to include it on *Song of Joy* little did we know that "Muskrat Love" would become one of the most polarizing hits of our entire career; people either loved it, or they absolutely *hated* it. Still it became our third biggest-selling hit single after "Love Will Keep Us Together" and "Do That to Me One More Time."

Delighted with the success of our first album, A&M gave us carte blanche to do whatever we liked on the second. Little did they know just how far Daryl would go in his constant experimentation with sound and pursuit of musical perfection. While I have always loved the beauty and emotion that music can evoke, such as in the romantic compositions of Rachmaninoff and Chopin, Daryl tended to be more technically focused. He preferred measured classical scores from the fourteenth century that are mechanically faultless and beautiful to hear but can be scant in emotion. However, the merging of our different musical tastes no doubt contributed to the distinct style of Captain and Tennille. I brought warmth, emotion, and accessibility to our lyrics and music; Daryl took those qualities and, through his scrupulous production methods, crafted them into a unique sound that was all our own. Really, when you listen to many of the songs on our albums, you are actually hearing the story of our real-life relationship as much in the music as in the lyrics.

At that time studio albums were typically created on sixteen multitracks, meaning that each instrument was recorded on its own track. Sometimes, one or two tracks would be combined to free up another track. The lead vocals, each individual instrument, and backing vocals were recorded separately so that each track could be fine-tuned before being mixed with the others to make a complete recording. The process could be as simple or complex as the producer desired. As producer for Captain and Tennille, Daryl could never resist putting something on every single track—using all sixteen tracks and combining many of them for one song! While I understood that producing was Daryl's territory, I sometimes felt that there were an awful lot of sounds being "blended" to excess. At one point I even joked that we should start calling ourselves "Kitchen Sink Productions" because it seemed that everything but the *kitchen sink* was being put into the songs. You could imagine what it was like later when we went to thirty-two tracks for our recordings! Fortunately, Daryl's instincts were usually correct, and after the song was complete, I'd understand what he'd been trying to do. But the few times that I doubted his judgment I didn't say anything because, quite frankly, recording with Daryl could be a stressful and sometimes volatile process. I never wanted to "rock the boat" during our long and complicated studio sessions.

My sisters Louisa and Melissa, who had again joined us in the studio to sing backing vocals on some of the tracks, often bore the direct brunt of Daryl's dictatorial management style. We both loved Louisa's voice, which had a cool, youthful, sometimes child-like, quality. Melissa had those wonderful high notes that the rest of us couldn't sing. But Louisa had never learned to read music and learned her part by rote, practicing it over and over until she got it right. Daryl had no idea how to coach or give constructive criticism to a singer or musician and could be extremely rude and impatient. He was incapable of offering the "spoonful of sugar" to make the medicine go down. Sometimes, if Louisa was having a hard time remembering her part on the backing vocal track,

Daryl would get so mad that he would kick her out of the recording chamber. "*Out*, Louisa!" he'd bark through the intercom from where he sat in the control room with the engineers. Humiliated, poor Louisa would leave the studio in angry tears. I'd always follow to try to comfort her, feeling terrible because I knew how valuable her voice was in our sound. When Louisa had recovered we'd march straight back into the studio to continue the session. I always admired that Louisa never gave up and am grateful that she held her head high and stuck in there, lending her unique voice to our recordings.

In between recording the album and continuing to make guest appearances on television shows, Daryl and I settled into our new house in Pacific Palisades. While I still shook my head at Daryl's increasingly oddball ideas about food—many of which seemed to have no scientific merit—I fully embraced the concept of healthy eating and became a vegetarian. We planted a large organic vegetable garden behind the house where I could pick squash, tomatoes, and beans for dinner; and there was an enormous avocado tree right outside the kitchen that seemed to be loaded with fruit all year round. Later we added a pool and a tennis court, which at that time was the sport *de rigueur* of healthy California lifestyles.

I loved having friends over for homemade dinner—all ingredients monitored judiciously by Daryl—with our two bulldogs snoozing beside a glowing fire in the huge stone fireplace. Immediately after dinner, Daryl, who was never one for socializing, would disappear into his bedroom and leave me to visit with our guests. Puzzled, people would say, "Where did Daryl go?" because he hadn't even said goodnight. I'd have to cover for him by saying something like, "Oh, you know Daryl . . . he just kind of wanders off sometimes!" Most of our friends already knew of Daryl's unease in social situations, but it could still be embarrassing for me.

In early 1976 I was stunned when we received an official invitation from President Gerald Ford and Mrs. Ford to perform along with the legendary Bob Hope at a White House concert for our country's bicentennial. In honor of this historic event, Queen Elizabeth and Prince Philip, along with Prime Minister James Callaghan and his wife, would also attend. With the leaders of the world's two most powerful countries together under one roof, security was extremely strict and everyone in our band and crew, including Daryl and I, had to go through thorough FBI background screenings.

I was nervous about choosing just the right dress for this very dignified occasion. It had to be something glamorous yet still respectful of the place and the people in attendance—nothing too beaded or sparkly, nothing low cut or slit up the leg. With the help of the designer and stylist Bill Belew, I finally settled on a simple, rather conservative gown in pale-cream chiffon. It skimmed rather than clung to my body and fell in soft layers all the way to the floor. Daryl wore a white tuxedo with gold trim and a white captain's hat.

As we made our way to the famous East Room to set up for rehearsal, I felt so privileged and awestruck to be in that historical place on such a special occasion. People all over America were celebrating the bicentennial, and here I was about to sing at the White House! But when we got to the East Room, my heart sank when I saw how small the stage was. This was a place meant for small acoustic performances such as a string quartet or an opera singer accompanied by a single piano. We, on the other hand, had six or seven microphones, all of Daryl's keyboards, and big amplifiers. How on earth would we fit it all on the tiny stage? And then, even with the speakers set at the lowest levels, I was terrified that we'd still be too loud.

But since the performance was just hours away, we just had to make it work. To make things even more stressful, our rehearsal time was very limited. All the while Secret Service men in their dark suits and earpieces stood everywhere, looking all around impatiently, watching our every move. Or maybe it just seemed that way to me. Once we had everything hooked up and started the sound check, which didn't seem all that loud to me, a Secret Service man came over and told us, in no uncertain terms, to "turn it down." So we did, but he returned to say, "Turn it down *more!*" So we did. But the volume was so low, I could hardly hear anything and wasn't sure if the levels were right. I was a complete wreck, and so was Daryl. Things were not going well at all.

We'd come up with a list of four songs to play, including, of course, "Love Will Keep Us Together." We decided not to include our only other hit at the time, "The Way I Want to Touch You," which seemed a little too risqué to me to sing at the White House. But as we struggled through sound check, trying not to anger the Secret Service, Mrs. Ford appeared; she was an absolute vision of grace and loveliness in a crisp linen summer suit. She greeted me with a handshake and a warm smile, saying how thrilled she and the president were to have us there. "Oh!" she exclaimed to me, "I hope you are going to play 'The Way I Want to Touch You.' Gerry and I love that song!" Taken aback, I mumbled something like, "Well, of course we will!" It was a direct order from the First Lady of the United States, so the song went back on the list! Emboldened by Mrs. Ford's kindness and enthusiasm, we finished sound check and completed our song list for the night, deciding at the last minute to add "Muskrat Love," since it had been such an audience favorite when we'd performed it at the Smokehouse and would be coming out on our second album. Smokehouse...White House ... people were just people after all, and surely the charming song would make our audience of dignitaries and royalty smile just as the club crowds had back in Los Angeles.

Later that evening after the audience had taken their seats in the East Room, Daryl and I took to the stage. I sat at my keyboard not eight feet away from the front row where the queen, Prince Philip, President and Mrs. Ford, and Henry and Nancy Kissinger all sat on little golden chairs. After the first two songs, I began to relax and enjoy myself, and I smiled out to the crowd as I sang. Queen Elizabeth was sort of dozing—her head listed a bit to the side (probably from jet lag and, maybe, boredom)—while her husband seemed to appreciate the performance as he smiled and tapped his foot to the beat. President and Mrs. Ford were also smiling and nodding along, clearly enjoying the show. As we started into the notes of our second-to-last song, "Muskrat Love," I was just beaming with joy at how well the whole experience had gone.

Then my eyes settled on Dr. Henry Kissinger, who was seated directly in front of me. He'd been sitting stiff straight through the entire performance, stone-faced with his eyes half closed, but the moment he realized that I was singing a song about two muskrats in love his eyes shot wide open. I could see he was not amused, and it only got worse for poor Henry. When Daryl started in on his synthesized muskrat squeals and trills, I could see the man squirm in his chair from what appeared to be sheer disgust. There was no mistaking that Dr. Kissinger wanted to be *anywhere* but where he was.

At that moment I wanted to be anywhere but where I was too. Sweat beaded my brow but I couldn't take my hands off the keys to wipe it away. "Chewing on bacon, nibbling on cheese. . . ." I watched as Dr. Kissinger turned around during the song to talk to someone behind him. What was he saying? Was he discussing an important matter of state, or was his contempt over being forced to listen to "Muskrat Love" so unbearable that he had to share it with someone? "Sam says to Susie, 'Honey, Would you please be my missus?'" Henry turned back around and continued to scowl with his arms crossed. All I could do was just keep singing and smiling until I thought my lips would split. "Susie says yes with her kisses. . . ." The room filled with Daryl's synthesizer solo of the muskrats squealing and warbling in ecstasy. I have never wanted a song to end more in my entire life.

We ended the concert with "Love Will Keep Us Together," and the audience applauded politely. President and Mrs. Ford seemed very pleased with the performance and thanked us graciously. Prince Philip, who seemed like a genuinely nice fellow, made it a point to say a few kind words, while the queen, who had probably dozed through the whole thing, gave us a regal nod of approval. Henry Kissinger, however, had beat a hasty retreat after the last song, and I never saw him again. However, throughout the years whenever I sang "Muskrat Love," I always dedicated it to "Henry Kissinger, wherever he may be."

When the concert was over, we all gathered in the White House ballroom for drinks and dancing to the Marine Corps Band. I was amazed at how loud they were playing, but no Secret Service was telling *them* to "turn it down." After such a nerve-wracking performance, it was a relief not to be the focus of attention and have a chance to really take in the surroundings and the fellow guests. But the highlight of the entire night was when President Ford asked me to dance. Neither of us was a particularly great dancer, but we made it around the room a few times without stumbling or stepping on each other's toes. President Ford was a delightful man, and I enjoyed the few moments we had together. And I was happy to have a chance to dance at all, because Daryl never would. If the President of the United States was my one chance to dance, you'd better believe I was going to take it!

A week or so later *Rolling Stone* magazine called us for an interview. It was the only time in our entire career that the hip rock-n-roll publication had ever taken even a remote interest in covering us. What I soon realized after speaking with the journalist was that word had gotten out that Captain and Tennille—the "squarest" group around—had had the outrageous audacity to perform "Muskrat Love," a song of "sexual innuendo" between two imaginary animals, at the White House. Apparently the chef Julia Child, who had also been at the event, had openly declared that the song was "inappropriate for royalty." It was actually quite humorous, when you thought about it. We just laughed it off. After all, didn't the country have a lot more to be concerned about in summer of 1976?

My father, Frank Tennille, young, handsome, and full of promise, when he toured as a big band singer, mid-1930s.

My mother, Cathryn Wright, when she worked as a fashion model in Dallas, Texas, around the time she met my father, late 1930s.

Mother, me, and baby Jane posing in our Montgomery, Alabama, living room for one of Daddy's many photo shoots.

A photo taken when Mother drove Jane and me from Alabama to San Diego, where Daddy was stationed during WWII.

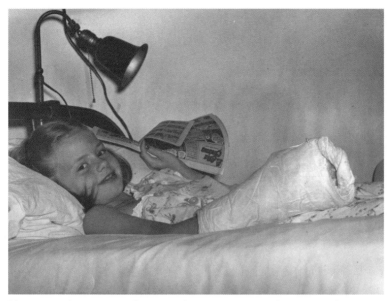

Me at age six or seven after one of the numerous painful surgeries to reconstruct my injured finger.

Me, about age ten, and Jane both sulking for the camera because neither of us liked the Christmas dresses that Mother had chosen for us.

Mother doing a live coffee commercial on her television show *The Guest Room* while my sister Jane pretends to shop in the background.

Singing with the Auburn Knights Orchestra, 1959.

Daryl Dragon, 1961.

Carmen Dragon, Daryl's charismatic, brilliant, and mercurial father, an Academy Award–winning composer and arranger who arranged many famous soundtracks and albums.

One of the earliest pictures of me and Daryl together, about the time we were touring with the Beach Boys in the early '70s.

Daryl and me performing as The Dragons at O'Shaughnessy's restaurant. This was the same place where a drunken St. Patrick's Day crowd accosted us because we didn't know any Irish songs other than "Danny Boy."

Probably the very first publicity photo of Daryl and me; you can see the adoration in my eyes as I gaze at him.

Our only wedding picture, taken in a tourist photo studio after we'd eloped to the old mining town of Virginia City, Nevada.

All four Tennille sisters recording "Love Will Keep Us Together" at A&M studios in 1974. From left: Louisa, Jane, me, and Melissa.

Winning the Grammy for 1975 Record of the Year. Joan Baez, at far
left, didn't hide her disdain, but Stevie Wonder seemed genuinely happy
that we had won.

Singing with Neil Sedaka, 1975.

With Bob Hope, greeting President Ford after our bicentennial
performance at the White House, 1976.

Daryl and me with the great George Burns on *The Captain and Tennille
Show.*

Trying to dance while smiling the entire time on *The Captain and Tennille Show*!

All four Tennille sisters onstage at the LA Universal Amphitheater when Captain and Tennille opened for Glen Campbell, shortly before *Love Will Keep Us Together* hit the Top 40!

Loved this T-shirt on a fan at the LA Dodgers game!

With Kenny Rogers filming the *Captain and Tennille in Hawaii* special for ABC.

My niece and coauthor, Caroline, at age six appearing with me on *The Captain and Tennille Show* Christmas special, 1976.

Loved this man—BB King! You can see the rare smile on Daryl's face; BB was his musical idol.

Captain and Tennille
promo photo, 1979.

With Cary Grant in the LA
Dodgers dugout, 1978.

Interviewing Lily Tomlin on *The Toni Tennille Show*, 1980. What a delight!

Performing as guest artist for a Christmas symphony with Maestro Barry Jekowsky conducting.

Promo shot of me in character as Victor in the national tour of *Victor/Victoria*, 1998.

Getting in costume for the first act of *Victor/Victoria* with my faithful assistant Becky.

Closing party for *Victor/Victoria* in Cleveland with my sister Jane. It was a happy end to one of the toughest years of my life.

In the backyard of my new Florida home with Smoky, Bebop, and Lula.
PHOTO COURTESY OF MARIE CRANMER

CHAPTER 11

By the end of the summer of 1976, Captain and Tennille had gone from playing nightclub gigs to selling millions of records, appearing on numerous television specials, and singing about lovemaking muskrats to a White House audience that included the queen of England and the president of the United States—all in under a year. While many people thought of us as an "overnight success," in reality Daryl and I had both been working hard at our music careers for over a decade. Sure, there was probably an element of luck in all our success, but we achieved what we did through years of working hard, overcoming rejection, and making very little money. The surge of fame was sudden and life-changing, and that summer after the Grammys, we thought we'd seen the height of it—until ABC approached our management team with the idea of creating a Captain and Tennille television show.

Variety shows, hour-long productions of music, comedy, and dance peppered with numerous guest stars of the day, were prominent on American television (along with sports, half-hour sitcoms, and gritty cop dramas). *The Sonny and Cher Show*, which had been a huge hit for CBS, ended in 1974 when the two host stars divorced. The search was on to find the next quirky couple to fill the void in the family-friendly variety show sector. Some of the executives at ABC had seen Daryl and me when we'd been guests on other television shows and thought our offbeat, "yin-and-yang" interaction could work on a weekly variety hour.

We met with Fred Silverman, Vice President of Entertainment for ABC, some other executives from the network, and our management team. The biggest sticking point during the negotiations was ABC's insistence that we include several comedy sketches in the show in addition to the musical numbers. They wanted content to be 40 percent music and 60 percent comedy, which Daryl and I couldn't understand since we were most known for our music and not our stand-up ability! Although we both understood that a variety show had to be a mix of both, we wanted the percentages to be reversed, with 60 percent music and 40 percent comedy. At one point, there was a dead standoff, and it looked like the deal might not happen. This agonized our management team who stood to profit handsomely from a Captain and Tennille national television show. They were frantic that we were going to kill the deal before it even got off the table! The lawyers for each side—who were the only ones enjoying themselves as their fees increased by the minute—pleaded, cajoled, and cursed back and forth. Finally we came to a sort of truce with ABC: We'd agree to do the television show consisting of 50 percent music and 50 percent comedy and skits. Daryl and I weren't thrilled, but this seemed a reasonable compromise. Somehow we would make it work.

So suddenly, in the middle of recording our second album, Daryl and I found ourselves signing a deal for our own television show with ABC called *The Captain and Tennille Show*. For me, the idea of having our very own television show was incredibly exciting. I'd always loved doing theater and had a strong background in appearing in front of audiences, going all the way back to the days of appearing on Mother's television show in Montgomery. I could hardly wait to start taping the first show, which was scheduled to debut in the fall of 1976 in the coveted 8 p.m. Monday night time slot opposite *Little House on the Prairie* on NBC and *Rhoda* on CBS. Daryl, on the other hand, had many more misgivings about the show than I did. I was far more enthusiastic about it than he was, but we had signed the contract and there was no going back.

I understood why Daryl was so hesitant. He was the quintessential smart kid in the back of the class, who slumped in his chair with his arms crossed, affected a "bored" air, and hoped that the teacher wouldn't call on him even though, most likely, he knew the answer. Daryl thrived not on being center stage but somewhere off to the side, and for most of our time as Captain and Tennille he'd been able to comfortably keep this position. But now he'd have to be a solid half of our television show, up in front right next to me with cameras focused directly on him. Until we started taping our show Daryl had never even seen a cue card, much less read one—which for the television world was an art form in itself. He once quipped that he was "learning how to host a television show in front of millions of people." And that was true.

Some of this intense discomfort could have been from shyness—after all, not everyone is born with the natural ability to shine in front of an audience—but some of it could have resulted from the painful treatment he'd endured as a child from his father. Carmen Dragon had been the consummate showman, handsome as a movie star, physically teeming with confidence and completely at ease as the center of attention. He could also be extremely critical of his children, and in particular Daryl, the son who'd shown the most talent of them all. Nothing Daryl accomplished had ever been "good enough" for Carmen. This constant scrutiny while he was growing up must have damaged Daryl's self-confidence and continued to haunt him even after he became a successful musician. Whatever it was, the whole ordeal of doing the variety show made him miserable, and I worried about him constantly.

For a show that was so lighthearted in tone, there was often a lot of tension on the set. We disagreed with the show writers about the kind of "banter" that they wrote for Daryl and me, which sometimes portrayed our relationship as argumentative or disparaging. This kind of humor might have worked for Sonny and Cher, but it wasn't right for us, and we refused to play along. There were many times we'd go in to rehearse dialogue and find that the tone was belittling, so we'd stop and make changes until it was right. It wasn't so much the "silly" stuff we minded—although poor Daryl hated when the writers made him crack jokes—because variety shows were supposed to be upbeat and fun. We were fine with making fun of ourselves while playing off our "square" image, but we never wanted to look as though we were putting each other down—even if it was just for laughs.

After a few shows, though, we naturally found our own type of on-screen identity, and when the live studio audience responded with great enthusiasm the writers backed off a bit. I was the gregarious, smiling Tennille always lovingly trying to pry a response from my awkward and stone-faced Captain. Although it was never his intention to do so, there was a real kind of genius in Daryl's reluctant television persona because it was so honest. He never smiled when he didn't want to. He delivered his silly lines with the exact same flat contempt that he felt, with no attempt to 'act' through them. He stared out at the camera with a perfectly blank, Buster Keaton–like expression. And guess what? The audience *loved* him for it.

In the imposing CBS studio building in Los Angeles, ABC rented a space to tape the show. They designed a moving set with an enormous neon "C &T" at the center and multilevel platforms that could change for each sequence. The production seems quaint now by modern standards, where everything is digitized and enhanced by computer video techniques, but it was pretty state-of-the-art then! The studio we were using was the very same studio where Sonny and Cher had done their television show. It was thrilling to walk the halls and see all the photos and posters of famous CBS TV personalities that had been there before us. My two younger sisters Melissa and Louisa had been recruited to sing backup and act in some of the show's skits. It was exciting for the three of us to have the chance to combine our talents for a television audience just as we'd done so many years ago on Mother's talk show back in Montgomery.

Once we started to tape the show we were off and running, and it soon became clear just how overwhelming and stressful doing a weekly variety show could be. I began to feel like Lucille Ball as "Lucy," in the famous scene where she tries to wrap individual chocolates in a factory while the conveyor belt speeds out of control. Each morning kicked off with a show writers' meeting to go over content, themes, and guest stars for the upcoming episode. Then I'd be off to practice the two or three choreographed dance numbers that I performed for each show, followed by rehearsal for the comedy skits. Before the week was up, I'd also spent hours with Daryl and the band practicing my solos and any duets I might be doing with a musical guest star. In between there were numerous wardrobe fittings with the designer we'd hired for the show—Bill Belew.

Bill, who had helped me dress for the White House performance, was a talented designer but also just a lovely person to work with. He always instinctively knew which styles suited my body best, and we spent a lot of time together discussing different options for me to wear during musical numbers, dance sequences, and comedy sketches. Bill would go to Paris a couple times a year to see the latest fashions and shop for fabrics, which he would bring back to make my show outfits. He drove a beautiful Mercedes sports car that had been a gift from his former client and friend, Elvis Presley. It was Bill who had designed many of the iconic bejeweled capes and suits that Elvis had worn in his Las Vegas shows. You can still see some of those fabulous outfits on display at the Elvis museum in Memphis.

On final taping day after the morning dress rehearsal I would shower in my dressing room and try to grab a bite to eat from the craft services table. Later while I sat getting my hair and makeup done, I would go over the script and rehearse my lines for the sketches and musical numbers. When our guest stars for the show began to arrive I would make the rounds to greet them. Daryl never wanted to go with me to greet the guests, so it was up to me to welcome them and make them feel comfortable and relaxed. And suddenly the producers were shouting for everyone to take their places. Ready or not, it was time to tape the show before a live studio audience.

For his part, between preparing all of the music for each show and learning his parts for intros and skits, Daryl also had an incredible amount on his plate. He had been very adamant that the Captain and Tennille sound would retain the same characteristics heard on our recordings and not be "watered down" as music often was on television variety shows. Just as A&M had, ABC agreed to our retaining control of the production of all our show's music. Daryl was often in the studio the night before a taping into the wee hours of the morning, prerecording several of the arrangements. He insisted that the music measure up to his standards and would not leave until he thought it was right. He'd be lucky to get a few hours of sleep before we were due back at the studio early the next morning to begin taping the show.

But despite the long hours and stress, I loved many things about making the television show. Our first episode aired in September 1976 with a sparkling roster of guest stars including Jackie Gleason, Penny Marshall, Andy Griffith, and Leonard Nimoy. I performed a duet of the Elton John and Kiki Dee song "Don't Go Breaking My Heart" with a young, up-and-coming actor named John Travolta. John had broken onto the scene in the much-loved sitcom, *Welcome Back Kotter*, and was just a couple years from superstardom in the disco smash film, *Saturday Night Fever*. Although his wardrobe advisor had dressed him in a tunic and tights—an outfit that made him look like Robin Hood—John was incredibly handsome with a distinct spark of charisma that made him irresistible. And to top it all off, he also had a pretty good singing voice.

Some people who watched *The Captain and Tennille Show* might remember the Bionic Watermelon skit. That had to be one of the silliest sketch ideas that our writers came up with, but Daryl loved it. A very tongue-in-cheek take on the popular '70s television series *The Bionic Man*, the idea was that Daryl and his sidekick, a "bionic crime fighter" watermelon, would have a series of absurd adventures together. Daryl got a huge kick out of creating the watermelon's voice. This was exactly the kind of "out there" humor that he really enjoyed, and amazingly a lot of our audiences liked it too.

And then there were the hat jokes. The writers found the subject irresistible—there was usually at least one hat joke in every episode—because by this time, Daryl's captain's hat had become his trademark. Daryl never removed his hat; his hair was thinning a bit and he was very self-conscious about it. Bill made a collection of hats for him in all sorts of colors and fabrics, each one more colorful and sillier than the next. But the hat jokes—delivered in Daryl's deadpan style—were funny because they were so terrible. "Who leaps tall buildings in a single bound?" Daryl would say, pausing to stare straight into the camera before delivering what was supposed to be the punch line: "Super Hat." Every time, the live studio audience would burst out in laughter and applause.

While we were taping *The Captain and Tennille Show* we were still working on *Song of Joy*. A&M was not at all happy that Daryl and I had decided to do a television show and had even tried to talk us out of it. They felt that having too much exposure would hurt our image, which, in their unspoken but obvious opinion, was already not "cool" enough. Perhaps they also worried that we would not put as much effort into recording or promoting the album. We tried to assure A&M that we were just as committed to recording *Song of Joy* as we'd been from the start, but doing the television show felt like the right step for our career, and we were going to do it.

The pressure was intense, but I wouldn't trade the experience of doing *The Captain and Tennille Show* for anything. The show gave me the opportunity to host and perform with some of my favorite stars. When I found myself doing comedy sketches with some of the greats like Bob Hope or Don Knotts, I felt like I was in heaven. Performers like these had honed their skills through years and years of practice, and having a chance to work with them was a complete joy for me.

For example, I've always been a fan of Dionne Warwick's crystalline, soulful voice and one of the most fun duets I have ever done was with her when she joined me to sing "He's Gone," a woman's twist on the bluesy Hall and Oates hit, "She's Gone." When we finished our duet to a standing ovation from the studio audience, Dionne's little son ran up to me. "Wow!" he exclaimed. "I've never heard my mama sing *that* loud before!" I took him in my arms and gave him a big bear hug. It was such a huge compliment!

Christmas shows were always a marquee event for variety television, and we made our Christmas 1976 show a full-family affair. My sister Jane flew in from Nashville and brought with her the youngest of her three daughters, six-year-old Caroline. Jane would once again join Melissa and Louisa to sing backup on some of the songs, showcasing all four Tennille sisters together on the show for the first time. I fondly remember the lovely, full-skirted silk taffeta dresses with ruffled shoulders and sashed waists that Bill made for us four sisters to wear while we sang the Beach Boys' "Little Saint Nick." It might have been 1976, but for that number we looked like real proper southern belles! I'm certain that our grandmother Edith, the quintessential southern lady, would have approved.

It was already planned that I would sing the song "Have Yourself a Merry Little Christmas," and I remembered that Judy Garland had famously sung it to her younger brothers and sisters in the musical *Meet Me in St. Louis.* Since Jane had brought my niece Caroline with her, I suggested that we have her sit on my lap while I sang it. Bill Belew quickly sewed up a sweet lace and satin dress for Caroline to go along with the Victorian-style dress I would wear. Caroline, who had never been in front of a television camera, was natural and unaffected in a way that a professional child actor would never have been, and the segment was quite touching. After the song I asked Caroline what she wanted Santa Claus to bring her. "I want him to bring me a bird," she whispered shyly, "A parakeet." Many fans wrote in after that show wanting to know if Caroline ever got her parakeet. She most certainly did; after all, how could Santa deny a little girl who made her Christmas wish known to millions of television viewers?

After a few episodes, ABC executives happily reported that *The Captain and Tennille Show* was performing even better than expected, taking about a third of over a hundred million viewers available in that Monday night time slot. But the stress was beginning to take a toll on Daryl, physically and emotionally.

During the rehearsal sessions, Daryl was often impatient and overly critical of the show's musicians in his effort to obtain perfection in a short amount of time. Although he didn't manage to reduce them to tears as he sometimes did my sisters and me, he simply did *not* have people skills. Daryl just knew what he wanted, and he was determined to get it no matter how long the sessions ran. So of course, he was not particularly popular with the musicians, and word always got back to me about how Daryl treated them. Other than trying to be very nice and encouraging, there wasn't much I could do for them.

But as someone who was subjected to Daryl's tyranny on a regular basis, I understood exactly how they felt.

CHAPTER 12

THE TWO-WEEK HIATUS FROM TAPING *THE CAPTAIN AND TENNILLE Show* couldn't have come soon enough. Even though I enjoyed the process, I was completely drained from the incredible amount of energy it took to get the show done every week. Just as wearing to me was trying to rally Daryl enough so he could get through the week himself. I was constantly trying to coax him through the busy week of preparation before we taped an episode, making sure he was emotionally supported enough to do his responsibilities, and frantically working on my own. I also worried about Daryl's behavior during the taping of the show. I prayed that he would make it through without an incident, while at the same time I tried to project a happy, confident face to the camera. But no amount of coaxing and flattering made a difference to Daryl's dislike of having to perform on our show. It didn't matter that the show was a hit. It didn't matter that Daryl's aloof personality, in sharp contrast to mine, had the unintended effect of making people hang on the edge of their seats for the few words he'd actually speak. It didn't matter that, despite his own determination not to play along, Daryl inadvertently created a distinct, if cryptic, television persona that fascinated our fans for years to come.

Something else drastically changed our lives when *The Captain and Tennille Show* aired. Our music first gave Captain and Tennille recognition, but our TV show propelled us to a new level of visual, all-encompassing fame. It's hard to imagine such a thing now in a world of seemingly unlimited entertainment choices and the instant connection through social media, but in 1976 there were only a few ways that people had access to their favorite stars: mainly radio, movies, and television. When our show premiered, there were only three major networks available on American

television: ABC, NBC, and CBS. *The Captain and Tennille Show*
was broadcast into over thirty-three million homes every week.
As a result, Daryl and I became instantly recognizable.

This wasn't as much of a concern for Daryl, who preferred to
stay at home when he wasn't cloistered away in the studio, but
the invasion of privacy came as a complete shock to me. Before
the TV show, even when Captain and Tennille had many hits
on the radio, my life was still relatively "normal," and I could go
out in public with only the occasional fan recognizing me either
from our album covers or guest appearances on talk shows such as
The Dick Clark Show and *The Tonight Show*. When you are a five-
feet-eleven-inches-tall woman with a rather distinctive speaking
voice, it's hard not to stand out in any situation. But when I began
appearing weekly on TV, people immediately noticed me everywhere I went.

One of my favorite ways to unwind has always been to spend
an afternoon shopping, all by myself. When the weather was
good, as it so often is in southern California, a day spent out in
the fresh air, wandering the shops and boutiques, was the perfect
remedy to a long, strenuous week of recording or taping. I loved
to browse the shops for a few hours before selecting a place to
have lunch, where I'd read a book and savor being alone with
my thoughts while I ate. When *The Captain and Tennille Show*
became a network hit just weeks after its debut, I realized that I'd
have to choose a different pastime if I wanted to relax.

I don't want to give the idea that I was resentful of the fame
that came with our success, something that Daryl and I had
worked so hard for so many years to achieve. But now that it had
finally arrived, reality was pretty overwhelming. It was thrilling
that the TV show had added a new, relatable dimension to Captain and Tennille. I loved knowing that our fans took so much
pleasure in the music, the celebrity guests, and the overall feel-
good ethos that we strove to share with them through *The Captain and Tennille Show*. But when you appear in millions of living

rooms every week, some people begin to think they really "know" you and will sometimes stray over the boundaries of accessibility. I came to understand how that could happen, especially after I was a guest on *The Rosie O'Donnell Show* in 1997 along with Katie Couric and Miss Piggy. By that time I had watched Katie so often on the news that I had to keep reminding myself that although we were chatting amicably together on the sofa like old friends, I did not actually know her, and she did not know me!

I woke up on the first day of the break absolutely giddy with the idea of having nowhere to be. The entire day was all mine to do whatever I wanted! And what better reward for all that hard work, I thought, than to go shopping, especially now that I had some money to spend? But something was different. I noticed that people in the stores were staring at me, whispering with their friends, and even following me around. I thought for sure I'd be safe when I went into a dressing room at Saks Fifth Avenue to try on clothes. But a brazen fan jerked the curtain open and demanded an autograph, while I stood there half-naked! For someone who had always cherished her privacy, this type of blatant disregard for it by a complete stranger was shocking. And it was just the start of what was to come.

After literally being "exposed" in the dressing room, I fled the store. Taking refuge inside a quiet restaurant where I had often dined alone, I sat down with my book for what I hoped would be a peaceful lunch. But within minutes, I noticed the other diners turning to stare, and the kitchen staff coming out of the back to look at me. People would approach my table and say, "You're Toni Tennille! Do you mind if I get your autograph?" Always wanting to please, I'd answer, "No, I don't mind." Fans would want to talk and ask questions as my book sat unread and my food grew cold on the table. At some point I would say, "It's been so nice talking to you, but I really need to eat now!" And after they walked away, I felt as though I'd angered them by asking for some personal space.

The thought of spending our coveted two-week break hiding inside the house was unbearable, and I was desperate for a diversion after so many months taping the show. Daryl would have been fine just staying at home, but I wanted to go where I could completely leave show business behind and forget being "Captain and Tennille" for a while. "Daryl," I finally said. "If I don't get away from LA, I'm going to go insane!" We decided that the only option was to leave the country and go where people wouldn't recognize us. I had seen pictures of Stanley Park in Vancouver, Canada, and the vision of those beautiful pine forests edged by the sapphire-blue waters of Vancouver Harbor and English Bay symbolized the exact kind of tranquility I was looking for. I pictured the two of us hiking through the miles of wooded trails and riding bikes along the water—the perfect balm for two overworked, stressed souls! We booked a suite at a luxurious hotel near the park and flew off to Canada, anticipating a peaceful couple of weeks of anonymity. We would be just Toni and Daryl, two ordinary people spending time together on a romantic and rejuvenating vacation.

What we didn't realize was that *The Captain and Tennille Show* was also being aired in Canada. Word quickly got out that we were in town, and fans started to camp out in the hotel lobby. Some of them actually sat on the floor in the hallway outside our room, waiting for us to come out. If I looked out the hotel window someone down in the crowd would spot me and begin yelling and waving frantically. Even when the hotel tried to keep them off the premises, the moment we stepped outside people would crowd around, demanding autographs, taking photos, and wanting to touch us. Fans screamed and shoved each other trying to get access, and when we finally escaped into a waiting taxi, they pressed their bodies against the glass to see inside. I just couldn't understand why people would behave like this; I had my idols, too, but there was no way I'd ever act that way if I met them! I'll never understand how celebrities today can keep their sanity with the paparazzi attempting to invade their lives in even the most private of circumstances. For me, the experience in Vancouver was terrifying and one that I wasn't at all prepared for. So much for quiet hikes through beautiful Stanley Park.

There was no way we could stay in Canada, so we decided that if we were going to have any kind of vacation we would have to leave North America. I had always wanted to see Scotland, so, without taking into consideration that the weather there was horrible in March, we flew to Edinburgh. We landed in a city besieged by sleet and freezing temperatures, but we were immediately warmed by the realization that no one recognized us. After a couple of days spent sightseeing, I said to Daryl, "It's just too cold here . . . Let's go someplace warm!" Italy seemed an obvious choice, so we left icy Scotland behind and flew to Rome, which, while not exactly balmy that time of year, was much more comfortable.

It wasn't only my cold fingers and feet that I was eager to thaw in the crooked, sunlit streets of Rome. Daryl and I were still in the early years of our marriage and, although we spent most of our time together, I still didn't feel as though we had made a true connection. *Perhaps,* I thought, *the tidal wave of sudden fame, and the strenuous mechanics required to maintain it, had starved out the intimacy that two people in love are supposed to have.* There was no denying that together we had great chemistry; it had ignited our musical collaboration into hits and our television show into primetime gold. After years of struggling to "make it," we were finally reaching our wildest dreams. But, despite all that we had accomplished together, I couldn't shake the feeling that I was somehow still "auditioning" for Daryl's love. In the afterglow of our whirlwind success, Rome seemed like the perfect setting for me to finally win the role I coveted in Daryl's heart.

Rome was everything I had imagined it to be. We stayed at the five-star Hotel Hassler, perched magnificently at the top of the famed Spanish Steps. The Eternal City of Rome spread outside our hotel balcony in a riotous jumble of wedding-cake palaces, elaborate fountains spewing water three stories into the air, and crumbling ruins made all the more beautiful for their decay. The cobblestone streets were alive with music, lights, arched bridges, and row after row of exquisite shops and restaurants—and I wanted to explore every inch of it. Best of all, just as in Scotland, the only people in Rome who recognized us were the occasional American tourists. Maybe, I thought, far away from the demands of our professional lives, we had finally found a place to continue the path of discovering each other as husband and wife and not just music partners.

But one of the first discoveries I made was that Daryl's idea of an Italian vacation was far different from mine. It shouldn't have come as a surprise, but if I had hoped that being in a city legendary for its fine cuisine would loosen Daryl's draconian eating habits, I was sorely mistaken. He managed to find what was probably the only health-food restaurant in Rome, and that was where he insisted we eat all of our meals. He refused to eat pasta made with white flour—and here we were in Italy, where everything was made with white flour! While other couples dined on terraces overlooking the river or inside beautifully lit cafés, eating wonderful Italian food and drinking wine, we would trudge up dark, narrow stairs to the health-food place, located on the second floor of a dilapidated building, where Daryl could get his whole wheat pasta and bland, steamed vegetables. When I tried to coax him into trying something else he angrily refused, insisting that the food in other places wasn't healthy enough. Daryl, always terrified about his health, was absolutely convinced that eating even a little bit of the "wrong" food would give him some terrible disease. And there was no convincing him otherwise. His irrational idea about food was just one of Daryl's many eccentricities that made life with him so difficult for me. There was also the hat.

Long before it became his signature as the Captain, wearing a hat had become an obsession to Daryl. He was extremely self-conscious when he began to lose his hair in his thirties, and he started to wear hats to hide the hair loss. Since being crowned "The Captain of the Keyboards" from his days playing with the Beach Boys, the nickname had taken on a life of its own and gave Daryl the perfect excuse to never be without a hat on his head. This became a problem whenever we wanted to go to a place where it was expected that gentlemen not wear hats, like fine restaurants. Sometimes they would permit him to keep his hat on, since he was "The Captain," but it was always very embarrassing for me. One time we were supposed to meet someone for an important business lunch at the Polo Lounge in the Beverly Hills Hotel, a very exclusive establishment where hats were not allowed. They didn't care who Daryl was; if he wouldn't remove his hat, he wasn't coming in. So, we had to hastily make arrangements to meet where Daryl could keep his hat on. I was absolutely mortified.

In the mid-'70s, when we began making money, Daryl decided to get hair transplants. At that time, the procedure required that pieces of the person's own scalp be cut away and grafted onto the places that were balding. I was surprised that Daryl, who was so paranoid about anything that could possibly jeopardize his health, would ever consider going under the knife for cosmetic reasons. But I was very supportive, hoping that the procedure would be a success and finally put an end to his obsession about his hair loss. *Maybe,* I thought, *we could actually go through life without having to deal with the hat situation!*

The doctor warned us that several surgeries would be required before the grafted hair took to the scalp and looked natural. After the first surgery, Daryl emerged with his head full of small, painful holes with clumps of hair implanted in each one. A few weeks later, the implanted hair died and fell out, as the doctor said it would, and Daryl would have to wait until the new growth came in. Once it did, another surgery would take place to fill new implants in other bald areas on the scalp.

The problem was, after the first surgery Daryl became spooked and refused to follow through with the rest. His scalp now looked worse than it ever had before, with the sparse plugs of transplanted hair poking up in random spots. After that, he hardly ever took his hat off, even at home, because he didn't even want *me* to see him without a hat! What had already been a very frustrating situation now became even worse. Daryl's refusal to remove his hat had kept us from doing many things that "normal" people do. But while I could reluctantly pass up eating at a fancy restaurant, there was one place in Rome we weren't able to go that I still, to this day, can't get over.

I remember standing outside the gates of Vatican City, with its gilded domes topped with their multi-colored flags visible over the stone walls, and realizing that Daryl was being absolutely serious when he said he wouldn't take off his hat to visit the holy city. There we were, just steps away from some of the greatest museums and cathedrals in the world, including the Sistine Chapel, which I'd always dreamed of seeing with my own eyes. But, because Daryl absolutely refused to take off his hat for a few hours, I wasn't able to go in. After another glum meal of brown rice at the dank health-food restaurant, we headed back to the hotel.

Other women might have been furious that their husband was acting so selfishly. Some might have even said, "Well, to hell with you. Stay in the darn hotel—I'm going to see the Sistine Chapel by myself!" Of course, a part of me realized that most of the time Daryl only thought of his own wants and needs. But any thought of standing up for myself was stymied by my determination to make Daryl happy. I just had to keep on being the supportive wife and partner who sang the love songs, smiled on the television, and ignored all the glaring flaws in our relationship.

On our last night in Rome, while Daryl slept in the bed behind me, I stood at the open window watching people move back and forth on the torchlit Spanish Steps. Many were couples walking arm in arm with their heads bent close together, who whispered and laughed as though love were some great secret that they alone shared. Even from a distance, I could see the stark difference between those lovers and my own relationship with Daryl. Our absence of intimacy and tenderness was thrown in full relief against a city ablaze with passion. I finally had everything I'd always wanted yet here I was, unable to sleep, standing at a darkened window, and once again feeling more alone than ever before.

When our vacation was up, we flew back to California to resume taping *The Captain and Tennille Show*. What should have been a time of fun and relaxation had actually taken a huge emotional toll on me, and I arrived back home looking forward to having the distraction of work to take my mind off my relationship with Daryl. I was still madly in love with him, and, as people tend to do when they are in love, I figured that as long as I kept being supportive, my efforts would eventually pay off. I truly believed that Daryl just needed someone who could look past the aloof, complicated man and see the sad, lonely child within . . . the little boy who just wanted to be loved and understood. The key to my husband's love was just beyond my fingertips, waiting for me to find it. And I still had a lifetime left to search.

CHAPTER 13

We should have just stayed home in California during our season break.

By the time Daryl and I had flown home from Europe, recovered from jet lag, and caught up on business matters, and preproduction meetings for our show, it felt like there had been no vacation at all. After about three weeks of taping, Daryl came to me one evening after we'd come home from the studio. It had been a particularly frustrating day of preparation for the next show. "I can't take it anymore," he said. "I don't want to continue with the show." I knew that when Daryl made up his mind about something, that was it, and there was no talking him out of it. Daryl was done with the silly skits, the hat jokes, the grueling work schedule. Even though I really wanted to continue with the show, I felt there was no choice but to support his decision. *The Captain and Tennille Show* could not exist without the Captain. "OK," I said. "Well, I guess we need to call Fred Silverman and tell him we're quitting the show."

Fred, ABC's vice president, wasn't going to let us go without a fight. He was stunned that we wanted to quit.

"But you're only halfway through the season," he exclaimed over the phone from his office in New York. "And it's a hit! No one quits a show when it's a hit." We told Fred that we would honor our contractual obligations to finish the season, but that we didn't want to sign on for a second season. Fred persuaded us to fly out to New York to talk things over, though I doubted it would make any difference.

Once we arrived in New York Fred sat us down and got right to the point. "What do we have to do to make you change your mind?"

"Well," I said. "More emphasis on music." That was the only thing that I knew might sway Daryl to continue the show. "We want more music and less comedy."

Fred moaned and argued and wrung his hands, but in the end he started to give in. We knew we were getting somewhere when Fred asked us if it would help if he got us a different producer for the second half of the first season. In fact, he told us, he had already been thinking along those lines and had prepared a list of potential producers to replace Bob Henry, who had been producing the show since it started. Bob was a classic "old school" television guy and tended to stock the show with older stars like Jackie Gleason and Andy Griffith. They were incredibly esteemed and wonderful entertainers but weren't really what the younger viewers were interested in. Fred agreed that we needed to find someone who would foster not only a more music-focused show but one that would include some of the newer acts coming onto the scene. *The Captain and Tennille Show* already had a solid family-centric following, as most television variety programs did, but we had hoped a stronger emphasis on Top 40 music would appeal to a younger audience as well. As we went down the list of proposed producers one name immediately jumped out: Dick Clark. We didn't even have to think about it. Dick, we told Fred, was the man we wanted.

It almost seemed that Fred, a true genius in the art of handling even the most difficult talent, had done what I believed would be impossible: He convinced Daryl to give the show another chance. ABC agreed to lessen the show's emphasis on comedy and increase the focus on music. And although Dick Clark had never produced a big television variety series, Fred gave us a true gift when he suggested him for the job. With Dick's youthful and visionary approach to the merging of television and music, Daryl and I hoped that our show could finally be the way we wanted it. By the time we left New York, I was feeling optimistic enough to think that there just might be a second season of *The Captain and Tennille Show* after all.

Dick Clark's entry as the new producer for the remainder of the first season was like a breath of fresh air. Although Dick had never produced a television variety show before, he had already proven to be a mastermind when it came to the art of channeling current music trends through a television format. And he was as charismatic in real life as he was on TV, full of new ideas and invigorating energy that recharged the entire crew. Already a household name through his own decades-long turn as host and producer of *American Bandstand*, Dick had become a sort of genial but cool "voice of reason" between the rapidly expanding youth culture and their perplexed parents, earning the respect of both sides. He seemed the perfect person to help update the show, and even more important to me, make it one that Daryl might actually enjoy doing. And just as important, Dick seemed to "get" Daryl. He wasn't intimidated by Daryl's abrupt manner and knew how to work with him in ways other people had never been able to.

The focus back to music was a huge relief for my sisters Louisa and Melissa. I'd wanted them to be involved in the show as much as possible as backup singers, actors, and dancers. Melissa's husband, Andy, who was a very talented singer, also joined the background cast for the show. Not only was it a way for my sisters to make some money using their natural talents, but being a part of a major network show had its perks. Louisa loved the ritual of stopping in at the Vidal Sassoon salon near the studio where she'd be whisked right in to have her hair, makeup, and nails done before heading into work. My sisters each had designated, reserved parking spots with their names on them at the studio lot.

It was exciting to see who might appear in the studio commissary where we ate our lunch. Once when we were rehearsing for a *Tonight Show* appearance at NBC studios in Burbank, Louisa and I walked into the commissary to grab a bite to eat. All of a sudden I noticed she was behaving strangely. "Oh my

God," she whispered, pointing slyly to a group of people sitting at a nearby table. "Look who's in here!" I looked, but I had no idea who she was talking about. It turned out that the people she was referring to were some of the big stars of the NBC soap *Days of Our Lives*. I, who had never watched a single episode of a soap opera in my life, had no idea who these people were. But Louisa was a huge fan of the series, and she could hardly believe she was actually seeing her favorite characters and the actors who played them casually eating their salads and tuna fish sandwiches just like everyone else.

As singers and actors Louisa and Melissa could each hold their own without issue. But dancing? That was another story. Taping the very first show had been a nightmare for them. Both were expected to get up and dance on wobbly platforms, a challenging task for even experienced dancers, but sheer terror for those who were not trained. Other than taking ballroom lessons as adolescents (insisted upon by Mother) and boogying at discos with their friends, neither of my sisters had ever had any real dance experience.

Rehearsals for that first show became miserable and dreaded affairs for everyone involved. The choreographer, pressed for time and not used to dealing with untrained dancers, would become impatient when he had to stop rehearsal to go through the steps one by one, while the professional dancers hired for the show stood on the sidelines rolling their eyes. Even the most rudimentary of dance vocabulary had to be explained, such as "5, 6, 7, 8," the most basic dance count-off of all! "What the hell happened to 1, 2, 3, 4?" Louisa muttered to me after she'd gamely stomped through a routine. I had a lot more dance experience than my sisters did, because I had studied ballet and jazz off and on since childhood, but the rehearsals were never easy for me, either.

Things were looking grim for Louisa and Melissa. The choreographer would bark out his commands, the professional dancers would all gracefully spin one way, and the Tennille clan would clumsily spin the opposite way, which often caused an onstage collision. As time progressed, Louisa anxiously confided to me that she sensed a rebellion brewing among the sleek pack of professional dancers. She told me they would gather off to the corner during breaks to smoke cigarettes, whispering and throwing venomous glares at her and Melissa. The dancers didn't behave this way toward me—at least not to my face—but it was obvious they absolutely loathed sharing the stage with us just as much as we hated looking like idiots in front of them.

Finally the dancers couldn't take it any longer. They went to the show's producer and claimed that having to dance alongside such horrendous, untrained dancers was making *them* look bad, and they weren't going to be made to look like fools on national television just so Toni's sisters could dance on the show! In the end the dancers won, which was a great relief to Louisa and Melissa, but the first show had already been taped so we had to use the footage. It is almost painful to watch even today. Performed to Kiki Dee's "I Got the Music in Me," you can clearly see that my poor sisters are doing their best to keep up with the professionals. And actually they did a pretty good job, which is difficult to do alongside the razor-sharp fluidity of real dancers. Especially when you know those dancers want to strangle you!

I was the star of the show, so I was treated much more gently by the dance team. Still it wasn't easy for me to get through some of the intricate steps. The choreographer discovered that there were about six or seven steps that I could do pretty well, and he would mix and match them for each routine. He would position the other dancers so that they whirled and kicked around me, drawing attention away from the fact that I was repeating the same few steps over and over. I also remember that I smiled a lot when we taped the dance segment, which I hoped would distract the viewers away from my feet. Using these tactics I managed to get through the number looking passably decent. But I was always very relieved when we had finished the dancing segments.

I'd hoped that the new focus on music and less comedy would increase Daryl's enjoyment of making the television show, but it soon became apparent that was not going to be the case. Even though the show had more music, we were still obligated to do some comedy sketches. There had been an initial glimmer of hope when Dick, in one of his twists of genius, brought in the talented comic and impressionist John Byner to write and act in some of the skits. John had the same kind of dry, oddball humor that Daryl had, and to my delight, the two got along great. Daryl had always admired the great improvisational comic Jonathan Winters, whose routines would often veer off into wonderfully weird and unexpected directions. Sadly we were never able to have Jonathan as a guest on the show, but John shared the same peculiar comedic style that Daryl could relate to. For the first time in skits with John Daryl seemed to be almost enjoying doing his part. Almost.

During the first half of the season the writers had produced very specific scripted skits that Daryl had to memorize or read off cue cards, which he hated. Daryl actually could be really funny—but it had to be on his own terms and at his own personal flow. John wrote some hilarious sketches for the two of them to perform that were almost improvisational in nature, with the humor being more surreal than slapstick. I never understood most of the skits that John and Daryl performed, but there was a kind of off-kilter chemistry between the two that the audience enjoyed. Except when he was playing music, the skits with John Byner were among the rare times that I could tell Daryl was having a fairly good time doing the television show.

But John Byner wasn't in charge of everything, and other writers on the show just could not resist making Daryl the object of humor—even during the musical numbers. In one particular situation, he was forced into being the butt of an absurd skit that became, I later realized, what was probably the final straw for Daryl. We had invited the soul-rock group, the Spinners, who had a huge hit with their fabulous song "Rubberband Man," to perform on the show. The choreographers arranged for me to dance and sing with the group. But they couldn't figure out what to do with Daryl. Instead of just letting him sit the number out, they concocted a hair-brained idea to have Daryl ride circles around us on a moving platform and pretend to play a kind of harp of large rubber bands. Daryl was livid at having to take part in this skit—which was just ridiculous even on a variety show level—and it took a lot of cajoling and begging to get him to do it. Some people might have been able to laugh it off and just go along, but Daryl was unable to do this. When you watch the "Rubberband Man" number you can see the misery on Daryl's face as he makes slow circles around the Spinners and me on his rubber-band cart while we sing the song. I really felt so bad for him. That's one instance I wish we'd put our foot down and said no. But when you're caught up in the whirlwind and nonstop pace of taping a television show sometimes it's easier just to give in.

Being on the TV show brought unwanted attention to another thing that Daryl was highly sensitive about: his eyes. Daryl was born with an eye condition called megalophthalmus, or "greatly enlarged eyes." When I saw pictures of Daryl as a little boy, he looked like one of the "doe-eyed" children painted by the artist Margaret Keane. I thought Daryl's huge, liquid brown eyes were beautiful—as did many other people—but he had been relentlessly teased about them as a child. The condition worsens with age and requires numerous surgeries to remove cataracts and control glaucoma. I'll never forget sitting with Daryl during one of his numerous eye examinations when the doctor breezed in followed by a gaggle of med students.

"Look closely," the doctor said to the students. "This is a condition so rare you will probably never see it again in your career." And they would all lean forward to examine Daryl like he was some exotic animal in a zoo. The fact that Daryl was also a celebrity only added to the fascination, and he hated being treated like a specimen to be studied.

The eye disease not only caused him embarrassment, but it also made it difficult to bear bright lights because his pupils could not expand and contract properly, so Daryl took to wearing dark glasses. Sometimes when we were in public a fan would rush up and *demand*—not ask—that Daryl remove his glasses and reveal his eyes. Rude strangers like this could be easily refused, but when the show's producers began demanding that Daryl not wear his glasses on camera it was a crushing blow. But even Daryl knew there was no way he could wear dark glasses on our TV show, so he relented, withstanding the painfully bright lights that illuminated our set as best he could. On television, Daryl's eye condition was very obvious. Once the show came out, we began to receive a lot of mail asking what was wrong with Daryl's eyes. For him it was like being the "different" kid in the school yard all over again—except this time, the school yard consisted of over 33 million people.

When the first season came to an end, Daryl told me he was done. He would not agree to do a second season of the show. This time I knew he meant it. ABC could not talk us into continuing. I had mixed feelings about quitting *The Captain and Tennille Show*. It had received great ratings, and we'd been able to invite some of the best music and comedy guests of the time to share the stage with us. Although it was exhausting work, I loved making the show—even the dancing became tolerable after a while. It was the accumulation of everything I loved about performing, with a weekly audience of millions. Where else was I going to sing a duet with George Burns, dance alongside the Pointer Sisters, or act in a comedy skit with Bob Hope? But I knew Daryl was over it, and that was the end. At least I would now be spared the difficult and emotional task of getting Daryl through each weekly taping without either of us losing our minds.

ABC wasn't quite done with us yet, though. We had signed on to do a series of three television specials for the network that would be spaced out over three years. The specials, which would be taped at different exotic locations, would be similar to *The Captain and Tennille Show* and would feature guest stars, music numbers, and skits. The first would begin taping in Hawaii in 1977. This would give Daryl and me some time to catch up on our recording obligations before we had to appear in front of the camera again.

Our record label was thrilled that we'd decided to give up the TV show. Maybe now, they grumbled, we'd be able to regain some of the "mystery" that we'd lost by being seen on television every week. The attitude is very different today; music stars easily cross over into television, videos, and even movies, but back then the music industry considered too much visual exposure to be a kiss of death for record sales. Now Daryl and I would be free to concentrate on just making music, which, as a couple, was what we really did best.

CHAPTER 14

SONG OF JOY, OUR SECOND ALBUM WITH A&M, WAS RELEASED IN 1977 while we were still in the throes of making *The Captain and Tennille Show*. Daryl and I had to squeeze promotion for the album in between our busy television-taping schedule, something that both of us were glad that we'd never have to do again once we'd finished the season. Three of the singles produced from the album became Top 10 hits; "Shop Around," "Lonely Night (Angel Face)," and the scandalous "Muskrat Love."

Over the years "Muskrat Love" has made repeat appearances on humorist Dave Barry's *List of Bad Songs*. I am a huge fan of Dave's writing and have read most of his books, and when I discovered quite by chance that he had listed "Muskrat Love" as one of his choices for top bad songs, I laughed out loud. I was thrilled that he even knew who we were! But in spite of its notoriety, the song had in fact made it to number three on the *Billboard* Hot 100 and number one on the Adult Contemporary charts.

With the success of *Song of Joy* and the cessation of *The Captain and Tennille Show*, Daryl and I were now back in A&M's good graces. We began planning our third album to be called *Come In from the Rain*, named for the title song, a heart-touching ballad by Melissa Manchester and Carole Bayer Sager. As with both *Love Will Keep Us Together* and *Song of Joy*, we included a song penned by Neil Sedaka, "Sad Eyes" and another he'd co-written with Howie Greenfield, "Let Mamma Know." The song "Don't Be Scared," by Bruce Johnston, also made the list.

And speaking of Bruce, he used to make me really cranky from time to time, beginning with the time he declared that Daryl and I were "too old" to make it and that my surname was problematic. In spite of this almost constant criticism of us, I always considered him one of the finest contemporary songwriters I had ever known. Bruce is probably best known for writing the Barry Manilow hit "I Write the Songs," but some of his other songs are, in my opinion, even finer: "Thank You Baby," "Disney Girls," "If There Were Time," and "Don't Be Scared," which we included on *Song of Joy*. The saxophone solo on "Don't Be Scared" was performed by the late Dave Edwards. Coincidentally, Dave had been a member of the Auburn Knights Orchestra when I sang with them back in 1960 and 1961.

We also included a song that I wrote called "Circles." Many of the songs I have written have been about Daryl, but none speaks more poignantly about my feelings of isolation within our relationship than "Circles." It was inspired by a short poem, "Outwitted," from the late eighteenth-century American poet Edwin Markham that I'd first read in high school. I immediately related to Markham's beautiful and simple words that said to me that true love has the power to slip through any barrier and change someone's life for the better.

Outwitted
He drew a circle that shut me out—
Heretic, rebel, a thing to flout.
But Love and I had the wit to win:
We drew a circle that took him in.

When I first got to know Daryl I was sure that I could help him open his heart and bring him from the perpetual darkness in which he seemed to exist. And I was completely certain that it wouldn't take him very long to respond to the warm light of my love. As time passed and his circle remained impenetrable, I still remained hopeful even though my confidence began to waver. Here are some lines from my song "Circles":

He drew a circle that shut me out,
He was afraid of what love was all about;
I knew that I'd be the one to unwind him
Then he could put all his fears behind him;
But oh, love and I we knew just where to begin,
Oh love and I we started his circle to spin
Oh love and I we drew a circle,
A beautiful circle, a wonderful circle
that took him in.

The poem, and the song inspired by it, summed up exactly how I felt about Daryl. Wanting to love, yearning to be close, yet always shut out by an invisible barrier that try as I might, I could never cross. "The Way I Want to Touch You," one of the very first songs I'd written about Daryl, had been full of hope and passion for what "might be." "Circles" also expressed that same hope, but I had come to the sad realization that it might never come true.

Despite my increasing loneliness in the relationship, I remained, and for the rest of our marriage I was a steadfast and loyal wife. When the news got out that there would not be a second season of *The Captain and Tennille Show*, rumors began to spread about the inevitable demise of our relationship. "Tennille Breaks Up with The Captain!" one headline blared alongside a photo of me at a party holding a glass of wine. The article gushed on that I had been seen "out on the town without The Captain," partying it up with my Hollywood friends.

Nothing could have been further from the truth. I didn't have any "Hollywood" friends, the newspaper probably got that photo from some industry party that I'd attended, and that glass of wine I was holding in the photo was probably the *only* glass I had nursed the entire night. The divorce of Sonny and Cher, which had resulted in the termination of their own popular television show, made Captain and Tennille an easy target for speculation.

In between recording sessions for *Come In from the Rain,*
Daryl and I continued to appear as musical guests on various
television shows. We began plans for a national tour of over seventy cities to support the release of the new album. Touring was
never my favorite thing, but it had to be done to stay on top of
the game as a performing artist. And there is no other sensation
in the world like feeling the response of a live audience who is
totally tuned into your music. It is a very physical, spiritual, and
intimate connection. *That* part I love! The actual touring part?
Not so much.

I have always been a homebody, preferring to live a quiet,
routine existence with my pets, family, and friends. I like waking
up in the same place every day and knowing where everything
is. Even when we were working on our television show we still
went home every night—albeit sometimes very late—to the same
house.

But when you are on the road, it's a constant grind of airports,
hotels, and long hours of waiting punctuated by sporadic bouts
of rushing to the next city, or going from one radio station or TV
station to another interview. I'd always get a burst of adrenaline
just before taking the stage, but after the concert there would be
another hour or so spent greeting fans or VIPs who were waiting
to meet us backstage. Only after we had met everyone in line, and
had posed for photos and signed autographs, could I head back
to the hotel, wipe off the makeup, and fall flat on the bed for a
few hours' sleep—knowing the wake-up call would come early
the next morning.

A full band and crew accompanied us on tour, and getting
everyone and everything to move quickly from one place to
another required an enormous amount of preparation and orga-
nizing. Sometimes plain old luck got us to where we were supposed to be on time.

For a short while we chartered a plane that had been previ-
ously used by the rock group Fleetwood Mac. I must admit that

being able to drive right up on the tarmac to board instead of having to go through all of the airport rigmarole was pretty wonderful. Daryl and I, our backup musicians, and members of our crew would fly together in the moderate-sized turbo-prop plane from city to city. We named the craft "Broddy Bounce," after the instrumental boogie song Daryl wrote for our first record, because the plane would literally bounce up and down like a kite caught in a windstorm! Louisa and I would grasp hands and close our eyes until the plane leveled off and resumed a smoother ride. We passengers always felt a little more humbled—and very grateful—when Broddy Bounce finally touched down safely at our destination. When I think about our flights on Broddy Bounce now, I realize that we really didn't know a damn thing about our young pilots, the plane's inspection history, how much experience the crew really had—not to mention how *very* expensive a private plane was! So it wasn't long before we were back to flying on the commercial airlines.

Just as he had done when we toured with the Beach Boys years earlier, Daryl would bring his own supply of food on tour in the same metal ammunition case he'd used back then. Can you just imagine trying to get through a TSA security check today with a locked metal ammunition case filled with food? Never in a million years would it work. But back in the 1970s, you could take just about anything you wanted on a plane.

Daryl had become even stricter about his eating requirements. By this time I was a faithful lacto-ovo vegetarian, meaning I ate dairy products and eggs but not meat, but Daryl had gone much further and was rapidly narrowing his list of "acceptable" foods. Some of his beliefs, such as the avoidance of white bread and sugar, which science has since validated, were way ahead of the times. But many other ideas were just plain bizarre. For example, Daryl decided one day that he wouldn't eat any purple foods— even organic eggplant picked fresh from our garden—-because he believed purple foods were "negative." It was quite convenient for him that purple foods weren't very common, or he very well might have starved to death.

As a result of his food paranoia, Daryl continued to seek out vegetarian health restaurants to the exclusion of all others, and those were hard to find in many of the cities we were playing. Dutifully, I continued to join him in the hotel room for meals of brown rice cooked over a portable hot plate while everyone else went out to the best restaurants in town—pizza in Chicago, seafood in Boston, or soul food in the smaller southern towns. Sometimes I would go out with our musicians and crew to have a somewhat "normal" meal after Daryl had retired for the night. We always had our own hotel rooms because Daryl usually just wanted to be alone. He liked me to come to his room and visit with him for a while; we'd talk and listen to the radio or eat the food he'd cooked on the hot plate. But I could always tell when he was ready for me to leave because a certain expression would come over his face . . . boredom maybe? Whatever it was, I'd take the hint that I was dismissed and go off to my own hotel room, where we'd end the night apart.

Daryl's possession of his own food supply often put him in a position of power when we were on the road. Sometimes we'd end up at a regional airport waiting hours for the plane to arrive. Many of these smaller airports had no cafeteria or vending machines so there wasn't a place to get anything to eat. Louisa clearly remembers a few instances on tour when she found herself absolutely ravenous when we were stuck at one of these airports. Daryl, who always had his cache of healthy edibles on hand, would "sell" her a banana for a dollar. I don't think he ever charged me for food, but after all, I *was* his wife!

My memories of touring are rather blurry since my life while on tour consisted mainly of airports, hotels, and whatever venues we happened to be playing. And there were always the constant visits to the local Top 40 radio and news stations for interviews, usually very early in the morning. The radio stations loved to hold promotional contests where fans could win tickets, Captain and Tennille merchandise, or backstage passes. One radio station in Texas held a "Best Hat Joke" contest and they asked Daryl and me to judge the entries. Other times, people would call in to just ask us questions. They always wanted to know about our famous bulldogs, Broderick and Elizabeth, who had stayed back home in California. Anticipating the interest in our two dogs, we had produced a video montage for the tour of them playing, rolling on the ground, and sleeping. The video would play on a big screen over the stage when Daryl performed "Broddy Bounce." It was always a huge hit with audiences.

Sometimes an invitation would come from other musicians and friends who had homes in the city where we were playing. The one I remember most vividly was when we were in Toronto performing at the Canadian National Exposition and were invited to a party at the folk-rock legend Gordon Lightfoot's home. I was thrilled because I loved Gordon's voice and the songs he wrote, particularly "If You Could Read My Mind" and "Beautiful," both of which Daryl and I had performed back in our nightclub days. I always felt that I knew Gordon's heart when I sang his songs; it is hard to explain, but his music touched me deeply.

Daryl, who had no interest in attending the party, stayed behind at the hotel, but I wasn't about to miss a chance to meet and spend some time with Gordon. In 1977 he was riding high with the success of his songs "The Wreck Of The Edmund Fitzgerald" and the sexy, bluesy "Sundown." Louisa and I gathered some of the crew, and we all piled into a taxi for the drive to Gordon's home on the outskirts of the city.

When we arrived at Gordon's beautiful Tudor-style home, it was crammed with people, smoke, and music. Gordon greeted us warmly and took us on a tour of the place—the highlight of which was the huge kitchen where at least ten raccoons of various sizes were wandering freely around on the floor and countertops as Gordon tossed them bits of food. Evidently, he let the family of raccoons in every night when they came begging at the kitchen door. It was very strange to see all those raccoons making themselves at home in Gordon's beautiful gourmet kitchen!

"My God!" Louisa exclaimed as we drove away in a taxi later that night. "I've never seen so many stoned people in my entire life."

I looked at her in surprise. "Really?" I was still thinking about the raccoons.

Louisa rolled her eyes. "Toni, those people were so high they were practically flying. There were drugs *all over the place!*"

"Where?" I said. "I didn't see any."

"Trust me," Louisa said with a knowing smile. "That was quite a party Gordon had going on there."

It was typical of me to not notice or think about people's drug use. It had come up before, when Daryl and I threw a Halloween party at our home and invited all of our friends and some of our record company business associates. I was a huge Los Angeles Dodger fan, so I decided my costume would be a Dodger's uniform. Daryl refused to wear any kind of costume and appeared just as himself, which was costume enough, I guess. Lenard, one of our backup singers whom we all adored and who stood over six feet tall and was covered with red body hair, arrived dressed as a ballet dancer complete with a pink tutu. He instantly became the star of our party.

When the people from our management company arrived, they seemed uncomfortable as they looked around the house and whispered to one another. After a little while, they said a hasty good-bye and left.

"Why did they leave so quickly?" I asked one of my friends. After all we had a big table of great food, a full bar, and a wonderful assortment of interesting people at the party. What possibly could have been missing?

"They left because they couldn't find the *cocaine room*, Toni," my friend patiently explained. "Once they realized there was no coke here, it was time for them to head to the next party."

"Oh," I said. Would I ever learn?

But the rest of us had a fabulous time at the party, which ended when we all (*sans* Daryl) decided to go roller-skating at the local rink in our Halloween costumes.

Music industry parties were ubiquitous, and Daryl and I both knew that some of our band and crew indulged in that scene. And, as this *was* the late '70s, sex and drugs were just part of the program. Louisa and Melissa, who were both younger than I was by several years—and a lot hipper—occasionally hung out with the crew and band, so they knew exactly what was going on. There were whispers about groupies and all-night goings-on in the hotel rooms. But no one said anything to me, and that was fine. All I wanted to know was that everyone could show up on time and do their jobs when work resumed.

The *Come In from the Rain* tour had kicked off in California and made its way West to East with venues ranging from theaters to sports arenas. Never, since touring with the Beach Boys, had we played for such huge audiences. Although the really large venues were exciting, I always preferred playing more intimate settings because I felt more connected to the members of the audience.

When we performed in some of the southwestern cities, I always made sure to sing parts of "Love Will Keep Us Together" in Spanish as well as English. I wanted native Spanish speakers to feel equally welcome in the Captain and Tennille family, and it was a great thrill to see the faces of those fans light up when we started in with "Por Amor Viviremos." Then they too could sing along with all the joy and gusto that only one's native language allows.

By summer the tour had made its way to the Northeast where, at one point in New York, the demand for tickets was so high that we added a third night to the two we had booked at the Westchester Premier Theater. Our show opened with a flickering wash of colored lights over a darkened stage, where a lone spotlight would illuminate me sitting at my piano. A second spotlight trained on

Daryl, who sat across the stage from me nearly invisible behind his mountain of synthesizers and keyboards. As we began the first song, the huge C & T logo behind us lit up, which sent the crowd into cheers of anticipation. Another platform toward the back of the stage lit up to showcase our background singers, including my sisters, Louisa and Melissa, swaying to the beat. As the song progressed, the rest of our band joined in, and we built to a crescendo of boogie keyboards, percussion, and harmonizing voices. We wove our way through high-energy favorites like "Shop Around" and "Mind Your Love" while touching down with softer and more romantic love songs like "The Way I Want to Touch You."

And of course, the audience would never have forgiven us if we hadn't included our more playful songs like "Muskrat Love" and "Butterscotch Castle" somewhere in the set. "Love Will Keep Us Together" was always the last song in the lineup, and the punchy, opening chords from Daryl's keyboards would send the audience into a frenzy of excitement as soon as they recognized it. As an encore we performed "We Never Really Say Goodbye," the song that Daryl and I had written together for the end of each episode of the television show. In later years we would always close with "Come In from the Rain," a beautiful and emotional song of love and friendship and one of the few for which I accompanied myself on piano.

I always talked to the audience throughout our shows, telling stories about the songs I was about to sing. This made me feel closer to the audience, as if we were friends having a chat about the music and not just strangers separated by a stage. If Daryl ever spoke at all—and it was rare—he'd usually mutter a few words into the microphone such as "Good evening" or "Thank you." But that was all it took for the crowd to erupt in applause and sometimes even a standing ovation.

Finally the tour wrapped, and it was time to return home to California. Daryl and I missed our dogs, and our reunion with them was an overjoyed romp of waggling bodies and face-licking.

I was happy to be home for a little while, even though our schedule after the tour remained full. There was barely time to catch our breath before we had to leave again for work. But this time our destination was beautiful Hawaii, where we would be taping the first of our Captain and Tennille ABC television specials.

CHAPTER 15

I HAVE ALWAYS TRULY LOVED THE HAWAIIAN ISLANDS. DARYL and I vacationed there as often as we could, mostly on the Kona side of the Big Island that is also called Hawaii. Everything about the place—the laid-back lifestyle, the liquid, poetic Hawaiian language, and the languid sounds of its native music—made me feel as though there truly was a perfect paradise on earth.

So I couldn't imagine a more beautiful location to set our first hour-long ABC television special. *The Captain and Tennille in Hawaii* show would feature music, special guests, and tours of the islands' breathtaking scenery. I wanted to share the beauty and history of Hawaii with our viewers and, hopefully, make them feel as though they were right there with us. Most of the special took place on the Big Island, but we also taped some segments on Maui. Maui's eastern side, known as Hana, is spectacularly beautiful with jungle-laced waterfalls that careen off cliffs into the crashing Pacific Ocean hundreds of feet below. Hana provided a postcard-perfect backdrop for many of the show's segments.

Our special guests on the Hawaii show were Kenny Rogers, fresh off the success of his self-titled album with the hit single "Lucille," David Soul who played Hutch on the "hunky cop" series *Starsky & Hutch*, and our old friend Don Knotts, who had been a regular guest on *The Captain and Tennille Show*. Available on DVD today, the special is a true snapshot of classic '70's kitsch with a Pacific Island twist.

There are some romantic montages of Daryl and me decked out in full Hawaiian garb as we stroll on beaches or picnic on a lush green lawn. Of course, comedy was a big part of the show, with Don leading a skit as a tour guide with a flock of befuddled Japanese tourists. Amazingly, Daryl even acquiesced to participate in a shot of me pushing him, fully clothed, into a pool below a waterfall.

The silliness didn't end there. Someone thought it was a good idea to have Kenny gallop on a horse into a field and dismount to sing his song, "Love or Something Like It," surrounded by a herd of cows. Come to think of it, I also rode a horse bareback along the Big Island's oceanside cliffs while singing the Billy Joel song, "Just the Way You Are." The segment made no sense, really, and was comical because I was wearing a *dress* as I rode the horse, but it was fun. David Soul, who appears like some kind of seventies guru in a flowing white tunic and pants, earnestly sings a love song as he balances precariously along a rocky cliff over the ocean.

In one of the weirder parts of the special, Daryl dramatically performs the theme song from *Close Encounters of the Third Kind* on an array of keyboards set up in the middle of a barren lava field on top of a mountain. When he finishes the song, the keyboards magically "disappear" and Daryl runs off, waving his arms and clambering over the lava rocks as though he is being pursued. That was Daryl's kind of thing, and I think it was the only segment in the special that he enjoyed doing.

My favorite part of the special was at the end when the whole cast came together for a luau on the beach at Hana to hear the sensuous melodies of the famous Hawaiian band Makaha Sons of Ni'ihau. Unlike the other musical numbers in the show, this segment was taped live. At the end, everybody at the luau happily joins in with the Makaha Sons to sing the Leon Russell song "Back to the Island," as the sky darkens to a dramatic indigo blue and an ocean breeze tosses the palms.

ABC aired the *Captain and Tennille in Hawaii* special in 1978 to stellar ratings. It was nice to know we'd been missed by our television audience—especially for me because I really missed making our television show. The second ABC special would be taped in New Orleans later the same year.

One of the things that had caused me anxiety during the Hawaii special was that I had to appear on camera in a bathing suit for a good part of the show; after all, the show's producers said, that is what most people wear on the beach in Hawaii. Throughout my career I always had a very small waist but was quite generously endowed below it; I'd constantly worried about the size of my "womanly" hips and thighs. This was before Jennifer Lopez, among other more recent stars, made those features not only acceptable but also sexy and desirable! For the Hawaii special, I convinced Bill Belew to design a sarong that I could wear tied around my waist to hide my hips.

The pressure for women in the entertainment industry to be rail-thin was relentless. I never became anorexic or bulimic, but for a long time I was miserable under the scrutiny of the TV camera and the dreaded "ten extra pounds" it could add. In those years, I kept a daily journal where, along with each entry, I would record my weight for the day. If I found myself a pound or two over what I thought was acceptable, I'd get very upset at my lack of "control" and would exercise and diet until my weight returned to the ideal number. It just kills me to think of all the years I spent agonizing about my weight, and now, when I look back at photos and videos, I realize just how slender I actually was. But I sure didn't feel that way back then. The fitted dresses I wore while performing were often cut high up on the leg and revealed every curve of my body. While it was a lot of fun to have custom gowns designed for me by great designers like Bill Belew and Bob Mackie, those slinky styles also revealed any and every flaw. It took a lot of hard work and discipline for me to maintain a "camera weight" of 140 to 142 pounds even though my five-feet-eleven-inch body *really* wanted to be a healthy 150!

While I was relieved to have the sarong as part of my bikini costume, I still wanted to lose a few pounds before we began taping the Hawaii special. Some show biz acquaintances suggested that I enroll in a kind of a week-long "boot camp" at a place called The

Ashram. Nestled among the Santa Monica Mountains in Cala-
basas, California, The Ashram had a rustic-chic "spa" vibe with an
eye-popping price tag. It was—and still is—a popular place for
models, television stars, and musicians to go before a photo shoot
or a tour with the goal of shedding as much weight as possible.

The Ashram was run by a team of Amazonian, grim-faced
Swedish women who worked with military precision to coordi-
nate a grueling regime of exercise, yoga, and "detox" sessions. The
day would begin at dawn when we "campers" would wake in our
dormitory style lodgings (no private rooms allowed!) to march
out into the chilly desert air for a sunrise yoga session. Breakfast
was half a banana sprinkled with a teaspoon of crushed almonds
and a dab of organic yogurt topped with a single orange section.
Then it was off for more exercise—relentless repetitions of squats,
lunges, and weights—and a session of yoga to "cool down" followed by a vigorous-to-the-point–of-being-painful deep tissue
massage that was supposed to work out the lactic acid from our
traumatized muscles.

Just as you were famished to the point of nearly passing out,
lunch would arrive in the form of a few leaves of spinach and raw
vegetables beautifully arranged on a white plate with a drizzle of
balsamic vinegar, along with a small fruit smoothie topped by a
perfect mint leaf. After a very brief post-lunch break, there was
a mandatory group hike miles up into the mountains. And this
was no leisurely hike to enjoy the stunning mountain views. The
Swedes would drive us like a herd of huffing cattle to the summit, always yelling for us to speed up. "Faster, ladies!" they would
shout. "Only de *ups* does de goods!"

Only the "ups" does the "goods." I will never forget that
phrase for my entire life.

After our hike we'd stumble back for an icy shower (it helps
with circulation) and a dinner that, just like all the other meals
at the Ashram, was soul-crushingly sparse but always exquisitely
presented. Afterward, it didn't matter that you were sharing a

room with a bunch of strangers because we all either fell face down on our hard single beds and went right to sleep or, due to starvation and exhaustion, began to laugh uncontrollably until tears ran down our faces at the sheer ridiculousness of what we called "Boot Camp without Food." Then just before dawn a loud knock on the door would jolt you from slumber and back into reality: "Up you go!" Out of bed we'd crawl, each sore muscle painfully stiff from overuse, to line up for morning yoga.

At the end of the week I stepped on the scale to find that I had lost ten pounds in a *single week*. Now that my mission had been accomplished, I rushed off to Hawaii to start taping the show before those ten pounds—which was really more a result of rapid fluid loss than actual fat loss—could creep back on. I do remember that I was so ravenous after I got home from The Ashram that the minute I walked through the door I devoured two peanut butter, banana, and honey sandwiches while standing over the kitchen sink!

But somehow I managed to keep at least five of the ten pounds off until we finished the special. I went to Hawaii, put on the bandeau top, and smiled and sang my way through it all. But I never felt comfortable about doing it, despite all my hard work at The Ashram.

Today when I see all the pictures of young stars on the magazines and tabloids, my heart goes out to them because I know the kind of pressure they are under. Even when I was in the spotlight years ago, the expectation to be skinny was as real as it is today. And it's even worse now, with celebrities being stalked by photographers even during their supposedly "private" moments. No slight pooch of a full stomach or a single dimple of cellulite is safe from public scrutiny.

There's no way I can look back to the days when I felt so obligated to be thin without thinking about Karen Carpenter.

I saw Karen around quite a bit during our A&M days, as she and her brother were easily the hardest working people on the studio's campus, with an almost obsessive dedication to putting out music. Karen felt a constant drive for perfection, coupled with intense shame about her perceived body image, which would eventually become too much for her to bear. Everyone knew that Karen had a serious problem, although no one seemed to know what to do about it. Anorexia and bulimia were problems no one talked about freely as we do today. Instead, these problems were to be denied or just plain ignored, as though they would miraculously go away on their own.

I'd never been close with Karen, but I liked her a lot, and we would often chat when we ran into one another in the studios. Once, Daryl and I went backstage to say hello to Karen and Richard after one of their Las Vegas shows. I leaned in to give Karen a hug and, as my arms closed around her, I had to stop myself from flinching. Under her long-sleeved, high-necked, velvet pantsuit, she was just bones. I felt as though I were embracing a fragile bird, not a full-grown woman. I was able to hide my shock, but the realization of how painfully thin Karen was really disturbed me.

Later, one of our sound engineers who'd also worked with The Carpenters told me that Karen *always* worried about her weight. The Carpenters had the same management agency as we did, and it was under their ruthless scrutiny that vulnerable Karen began to succumb to the idea that she was fat. I'd felt the same pressure from the management team, too, but not like Karen did. She compulsively dieted and exercised, a dangerous obsession that would eventually claim her young life and forever silence one of the loveliest human voices ever recorded.

While I was trying to resist pasta and peanut butter to remain thin for the camera, Daryl was continuing on a very different kind of food odyssey. During this period he was getting most of his dietary ideas from his "guru," an elderly Eastern European cellist named Michael. When I met Michael, he was well into his nineties and living on a kind of commune in the Malibu hills where he dispensed his thoughts and ideology to various devotees who would visit him almost every day. I went with Daryl a few times to visit Michael, but I couldn't understand what he was talking about most of the time. And what I *could* understand greatly disturbed me.

Michael had written many tracts that included his rather unsettling thoughts on things like eugenics and the idea of a "clear race." Michael believed that over time humans would evolve to become whiter and whiter until they reached the "clear" point where you literally could see right through them. Michael talked about the Lemurians, descendants of people from the ancient continent of Lemuria that sank into the ocean thousands of years ago, who still lived in caves and tunnels inside northern California's Mount Shasta. The Lemurians, he claimed, were of the advanced "clear race" and would come and go through the summit of the dormant volcano. He said you could always tell when these beings were on the move because a particular cloud shaped like a flying saucer—in reality called a lenticular cloud that will sometimes form over mountaintops—would cover the summit to hide the Lemurians' activities.

I don't think Daryl really understood what eugenics meant— he wasn't the least bit prejudiced. And I doubt that he bought into the whole bit about Lemurians living inside an extinct volcano. Daryl was really only interested in ideas that affected him directly, so he listened to Michael's opinions on health food and pretty much ignored the rest. But it didn't take long for me to tell Daryl that I wasn't interested in *anything* the man had to say, and I never went to see him again.

Daryl also followed the dietary ethos of Paul Bragg, a pioneering health guru who is now best known for the popular line of raw apple-cider vinegar bearing his name. Bragg had written a classic book called *The Miracle of Fasting* that preached a combination of a strict organic diet and regular fasting. Daryl tended to customize his dietary and health beliefs, taking a bit from one guru here or there and adding in tidbits from Bragg and other diet visionaries of the time. Some of it was practical advice, but much was just plain weird to me. And for Daryl the weirder the advice, the more interested he was. Just as he had vehemently believed that the twenty-one-day grapefruit fast we'd done years ago would "fix" our damaged genes, Daryl was easily convinced that similar health miracles could occur simply by eating—or avoiding—certain types of food. Inspired by Bragg, he did a twenty-four-hour fast once a week for most of his life, and he was convinced that it flushed out all his body toxins.

When we were at home, Daryl would control his meals down to the very last ingredient, but the times he agreed to eat out at a restaurant had its own headaches. "What's in this?" would usually be Daryl's first question, and before he would eat a bite, the chef would have to come out and disclose every single thing that was in the dish. He would do the same kind of thing when we'd go to a friend's house for dinner. I would become very embarrassed when he'd begin grilling our host about the ingredients of a dish that he or she was serving. I tried to laugh it off, and everyone would joke about Daryl being "the food police," but I hated that our friends were subjected to Daryl's food obsession.

And when Daryl was around, people were not safe to enjoy their own meals, either. "That'll kill you," he'd quip flatly whenever he saw a friend—or anybody—eating something that he disapproved of.

When we flew out to tape our second ABC television special in New Orleans toward the end of 1978, I was grateful that there were no bathing suits in the wardrobe. Our special guests included Hal Linden of *Barney Miller* fame, John Byner, who had worked with us on our television show, and one of Daryl's all-time favorite musicians, Fats Domino. Fats performed his classic hit "Walkin' to New Orleans" before being joined by Daryl on the piano to play the rousing boogie-woogie song, "I'm Ready."

Naturally, jokes about Daryl's captain's hat ran through the show, which culminated in a jazz funeral procession marching soberly through the streets of the French Quarter and a eulogy for . . . the hat, which is tossed into the muddy waters of the Mississippi. Daryl stands next to me, *sans* hat, as we say good-bye at the end of the show. How anyone convinced him to go hatless on camera mystifies me to this day. But I was sure that he was as miserable and self-conscious about displaying his bare head as I had been displaying my bare midriff.

Of the three Captain and Tennille television specials, the third, called *Songbook*, was the one I loved doing the most. This time, it was all about the music; there were no silly skits, so even Daryl was excited about doing it. I invited one of my all-time favorite singers, Ella Fitzgerald, to come on as a guest; getting to sing a medley of torch song classics with her was one of the highlights of my career. Ella was one of the loveliest women I have ever met, and the beauty of her voice mirrored the kind of person she truly was inside. I tried not to act too awestruck while we were together, but I couldn't stop looking over at her as we sang and thinking, *You're really singing with Ella Fitzgerald!* Daryl got to invite one of his idols, B. B. King, and the two performed a vibrant blues number with a full band, on a set that was designed to look like a real nightclub, with candles on the tables and the whole audience, which included quite a few stage hands, sipping real cocktails as they watched.

I think it was in 1976 when Daryl and I flew to London to film a Captain and Tennille special for the BBC. For the return trip we had the opportunity to fly on the Concorde, a supersonic passenger aircraft that flew over the Atlantic from the mid-'70s until 2003. Upon arriving at Heathrow International Airport, we were escorted to the Concorde waiting area, where everyone was served champagne. When we boarded, I was surprised at how small the interior of the plane was compared to other passenger planes. Someone explained that the body of the Concorde was built very thick in order to withstand the great pressure of traveling at high speeds and altitudes. The windows were very small, but when I peered out I gasped to see the curvature of the earth. We were flying at Mach two cruising speed, almost sixty thousand feet above the planet!

Shortly before the three and one-half hour trip from London to New York was up—a trip that typically took seven to eight hours—the pilots invited me to come up and sit in the cockpit with them to watch as we landed. This was of course long before 9/11, and the security rules on planes were less strict than today. I was strapped into a jump seat behind the pilots, where I had a direct view out of the cockpit windshield and could see the nose of the Concorde, which was pointed and curved downward like a bird's beak, drop toward the ground as the aircraft slowed to about three hundred miles an hour for the landing. It was one of the most exhilarating experiences of my entire life, and I feel honored to have had the privilege of flying on the Concorde.

After we landed at JFK, Daryl and I raced right over to our hotel, changed clothes, and then drove over to Yankee Stadium. There, I sang the national anthems for *both* the United States and Canada before the Yankees played the Toronto Blue Jays. And only five hours earlier, I'd been in England!

It was time to start work on the fourth Captain and Tennille album with A&M. But though I looked forward to getting back to the studio, I had some apprehensions. *Come In from the Rain* did not do as well as we'd hoped, and I had some secret concerns that our time in the spotlight might be running out. If that did happen, I was OK with it. We'd had a terrific ride, and at least we wouldn't go down in history as one of the many "one hit wonders" churned out by the music industry. Still, I felt that Captain and Tennille had at least one more hit left in us.

It remained to be seen if A&M felt the same.

CHAPTER 16

WHEN CAPTAIN AND TENNILLE HAD FIRST BURST INTO THE mainstream back in 1975, Daryl and I had been advised by a security expert on how to deal with the inevitable side effect of fame—obsessive fans. Rule number one was *do not engage* with any person who exhibited fanatical behavior. Any kind of response—positive or negative—will only fuel the fire. Daryl, however, could not resist the temptation to interact with some of the most obsessive of our fans.

There was a woman, probably in her later forties or early fifties, who stalked us at our home in Pacific Palisades by lurking on the sidewalk and occasionally knocking at the door. Once when we were rehearsing for a show at the Greek Theater in LA, I looked out and saw a single person sitting alone in the middle of the sea of empty seats. When I realized that it was the same woman, who had somehow slipped by security to get into the theater, the hairs stood up on the back of my neck.

Despite my objections, Daryl decided to talk to the woman so he could "reason" with her. He had security bring her backstage where she told Daryl that God had instructed her to have his baby. The result of their consummation, she earnestly explained, would create some kind of messiah-like being. Daryl thought the whole thing was hysterical, even when this same woman would make sudden appearances at the backstage door of our shows all over the country and would send him long, rambling telegrams in whatever city we were playing.

Two other women—a pair of sisters—also homed in on Daryl and me and kept at it for nearly a decade. Again, Daryl was the main attraction, and he only fanned the flames by talking to them. These women even moved to Lake Tahoe where we'd relocated after we left Los Angeles in the early '80s. They would station themselves at the local post office where we picked up our mail each day and descend upon us the moment we drove into the parking lot, snapping pictures and wanting to talk.

This situation came to a head a while later when I was alone in our Lake Tahoe home and glanced out the window over the meadow in front of our house. In the distance I could make out two figures standing at the edge of the field with binoculars and a camera pointed at our house. When I got my own pair of binoculars and peered back around the curtains, my blood froze like ice in my veins. It was the two sisters.

Terror quickly turned to anger. We lived in a gated community, so I knew the culprits must have jumped the fence to get inside. Immediately I picked up the phone and called my friend Carole, who also lived in the neighborhood, to vent my frustration.

Now Carole, who had heard me express concerns about these two women in the past, is a no-nonsense type of person and not one to suffer fools lightly. "I'm coming right over," she said. "And I'm confronting those two nutcases myself!" Before I could protest, she'd hung up the phone and was heading over to the house. Carole marched straight out to the meadow and told the two women that if they didn't leave immediately the police would be called. She also explained in no uncertain terms that if they ever returned, they'd be arrested for trespassing. Carole must have been pretty intimidating, because that sure sent those two running for the hills!

The women stayed away from the house after that, but even this creepy breach of privacy didn't stop Daryl from occasionally communicating with them. Several years after the meadow incident, one of the women showed up at the house we'd moved to in Washoe Valley, Nevada. Not suspecting a thing, I'd answered the knock on the door and there she was, clearly drunk and just as delusional. "I wanna talk to Daryl," she slurred. I slammed the door in her face.

"*You* get to take care of that." I said to Daryl when I stalked through the living room. Whatever he said to her must have worked because we never saw either of the women again, although I suspect that Daryl kept up his sporadic correspondence with them for a while.

Although he could have had anything he wanted from some of these fans, I knew that Daryl's interaction with them was nothing more than a few random conversations or phone calls. Seeing how far they would go and listening to the bizarre things they would say was just a fun little distraction. He was like a bored cat toying with a mouse, picking it up, and tossing it aside at whim. Perhaps the mysterious, emotionally cryptic persona that Daryl presented to the world gave these women a blank canvas on which to paint their own fantasies about what he was like. If so, it would not have been unlike the way I had viewed Daryl for so many years of our relationship, until I began to accept that the canvas would always remain empty.

Daryl and I were feeling intense pressure to have another hit record after the disappointment of "Come In from the Rain," which had sold well enough but hadn't produced any hit singles. Along with expectations from our record label, we'd also lost the "nothing to lose" kind of innocence you have while writing and creating music before success hits—and that naïve chutzpah is often what organically fuels the spark for hit songs. We needed to prove to ourselves—and to A&M—that the Captain and Tennille magic was still there. In 1978 we went to work on our fourth album with A&M, which we titled *Dream*.

I must say that the cover art for *Dream* was probably the most fun and weirdly glamorous we'd ever done. It was shot at sunset on the Salton Sea, an austerely beautiful shallow lake in the California desert. I loved the photo montage of me and Daryl running against a dramatic desert landscape—Daryl in a loose linen suit, me showing a good deal of tanned thigh in flowing lavender chiffon. That cover really did look like something out of a dream!

When *Dream* was released we were lucky to hit the charts once again, this time with a sexy tune written by our old friends Neil Sedaka and Howie Greenfield called, "You Never Done It Like That." Neil had recorded it with a fun, bouncy beat but when I sang it in this style, it just didn't feel right for my voice. I wanted something different, still playful but also very sensuous. Daryl went into his keyboard room and shut himself up for hours, playing the song in countless different beats. Finally he called me in and played what he'd decided upon. And it was perfect.

That was the way it was with Daryl—emotionally we were in a constant tug-of-war, but when it came to making music together we really clicked. He just instinctively knew how to make my voice and the songs we played sound . . . *right.* Through our collaborative efforts, "You Never Done It Like That" hit the charts. It became such a fan favorite that we usually opened our live shows with it, and once the audience heard the first opening notes they'd erupt in cheers.

But in my mind the *piece de resistance* for the album would be "If There Were Time," a beautiful song by Bruce Johnston that just begged for accompaniment by a full orchestra. Daryl didn't want to do an orchestra arrangement because he never wanted to be compared to his father, so we approached the legendary Academy Award–winning composer Gordon Jenkins to see if he was interested. Gordon had written classic and timeless arrangements for Frank Sinatra, Judy Garland, and Nat King Cole. Gordon's agent told us he'd need to hear the song before agreeing to work with us, so we invited him over to our house for a listening session. Nervously, I sang the song while playing the piano as Gordon sat on the sofa listening with his eyes closed. When I was through, he opened his eyes and nodded. He would arrange the song.

I decided that we would record "If There Were Time" live, just as Sinatra had always done, with a full orchestra in the studio and Gordon conducting. It came out sounding just as beautiful as I had imagined it would. But it was also extremely expensive.

When Jerry Moss at A&M saw how much the recording for that one song had cost, he was livid.

"Don't *ever* do that again." Jerry said. "Captain and Tennille are a *pop* group—and pop songs are what sell your records."

I was also sad about the way Bruce Johnston reacted to the way we'd recorded his song. In his typical blunt manner he told us that he *hated* it. Bruce was a brilliant songwriter who took great care choosing the exact chords for his songs, and what he wrote was always flawless. But Gordon Jenkins was known for changing the songs he arranged to his own liking, often substituting different chords to alter the emotional effect. Personally, I loved what Gordon did to "If There Were Time," but as a songwriter myself I understood Bruce's dismay.

Things were changing in the music industry. The pulsing new sound of disco was rapidly gaining momentum and would eventually intermingle with elements of soul and rock to influence legendary breakouts like Michael Jackson, Donna Summer, and later on, Prince. On the other end of the spectrum was the raw, angry sound of a new type of music called punk rock. Punk came crashing onto American shores in the form of a group of foulmouthed, tattooed, and leather-clad British teenagers known as the Sex Pistols. When A&M announced that they had signed the group—most likely believing that this was their way to stay on the cutting edge of music—it was a huge shock to the rest of us.

The surprise signing of the Sex Pistols was a major topic of conversation among many of the A&M artists, especially those who'd long been part of the "old guard." I was surprised when Karen Carpenter came up to me when we were both taking a break from recording and struck up a conversation about our new label mates. She was not happy. "It's *our* kind of music that made this label," she said. "What does A&M think they are doing? This isn't music; it's just noise."

I understood how she felt. Since 1969 The Carpenters had made a ton of money for A&M and had long been the superstars of the label. Now the focus had shifted to the extreme opposite of their gentle soft-rock sound. But I also understood that A&M wanted to go where music was going, even if I didn't particularly agree with its direction.

It turned out that A&M would get exactly what they bargained for with the Sex Pistols. After a bawdy press conference in front of Buckingham Palace to announce the signing, the band and its entourage went on a drug- and drink-fueled spree that ended with their trashing A&M's London offices. Less than a week after signing the group, A&M dropped the Sex Pistols' contract.

Around this time I received an offer to guest star on the hit television show *The Love Boat*. Comedian Billy Crystal and the lovely singer Marilyn McCoo along with her husband Billy Davis Jr. would also be guest stars on the episode. I'd always enjoyed acting and thought it would be a nice break from recording and doing our live shows. Since the day I'd met Daryl back in 1971, we had scarcely spent a day apart. I was starting to chafe for a little independence of my own, away from Daryl's daily regime of pessimism and need for control. What could be more fun than appearing on this popular and light-hearted show? I immediately signed on, excited at the chance to work without Daryl's constant scrutiny. Or so I thought.

When I received my script, I learned that I would play a private investigator who falls in love with the man she's hired to spy on, played by *Brady Bunch* dad Robert Reed. When Daryl learned that the script also called for an on-screen kiss between Robert and me, he hit the roof. To my shock, Daryl was adamant that I would not kiss anyone besides him—not even just a G-rated peck on a television show! Daryl told me that he considered my kissing someone even as an actress playing a part to be a form of cheating. Some people assumed that Daryl's objection to his wife kissing a fellow actor on camera was just an extreme form of sexual jealousy, but in reality it was something completely different.

To Daryl I was a possession, something to be controlled and left untouched by everyone except him.

In my experience, Daryl was never an emotionally demonstrative man. In fact, I can say without exaggeration that he showed no physical affection for me during our very long marriage. Occasionally I would go up and hug him, and his body would grow stiff in my arms. He would only respond to my embrace by cupping his hand and giving me a little pat on my back; it was the same kind of awkward, tentative "hug" you would give to an old aunt that you hardly knew.

The Love Boat's writers finally agreed to edit the scene so that Robert and I would turn away from the camera as we embrace for our "kiss," giving the suggestion that our lips are actually touching even though they aren't. The writers were gracious about the situation, but I was mortified at what I considered a lack of professionalism on my part. I thought for sure that the *Love Boat* people would never call me again, but thankfully they did. Not surprisingly, the next *Love Boat* episode I was on involved no kissing.

I also appeared on *Fantasy Island*, another very popular television series at the time. The story line for this episode played on my ability as a singer. My character, Susan, was a successful young singer who longed to meet the mysterious man who had written the songs that made her famous. When Susan finally does meet him in his dark and gloomy mansion hidden deep in the jungle (remember this was *Fantasy Island*, so there's a perpetual tropical theme in all the story lines), she discovers he's a hideous monster with a broken heart. But her love breaks the spell, and magically the monster is transformed into a handsome man who leaves with Susan on the next plane off the island, waving good-bye to Mr. Roarke and Tattoo before flying off to live happily ever after. I still get a residual for "Rainbow Lake," the love song I wrote and sang for the *Fantasy Island* episode . . . it is usually the impressive sum of a dollar and seventy-six cents!

While my true-life husband was in no way a hideous monster, I really was the woman trying to break through to him with the power of my love. Funny how life can imitate art . . . even when it's just the plot of a high-camp television show.

I had been fortunate enough to sing backup for several wonderful artists, most prominently on Elton John's hit 1974 song "Don't Let the Sun Go Down on Me." In 1979 Bruce Johnston, who coincidentally had also sung backup on that song, called me up and asked me if I'd be interested in doing a vocal session for the rock group Pink Floyd. Apparently the group was recording what they called a "concept" album at a studio in Los Angeles and had asked Bruce to put together the same assembly of singers that he had for Elton John. That group consisted of Bruce, Carl Wilson, the studio singer John Joyce, and me. I wasn't very familiar with Pink Floyd's music, but I knew they'd made a huge impact with their cerebral, progressive sound and were highly respected in the industry as true innovators. Intrigued, I signed on.

When we arrived at the recording studio at the allotted time early on a bright Sunday morning, we didn't know what to expect from Pink Floyd. Daryl was so curious about this mysterious band and their recording techniques that he accompanied me to the session. We were half expecting to walk into a haze of pot smoke and groupies lounging around, so what we found when we walked in took us by complete surprise. It was just the band—clearly sober and ready to work—and the studio techs. There wasn't a joint or a groupie in sight!

Dave Gilmour, who along with Roger Waters had founded Pink Floyd, greeted us with a smile and a warm handshake. He said that he'd seen the two of us make a guest appearance on the kids' television show *Kids Are People Too* earlier that very morning. I must have looked stunned at the thought of a famous rock star watching a kids' television show because Dave laughed. "I was up watching it with my kids while we ate breakfast," he explained. *So much for the wild rock-and-roll stereotype*, I thought!

The recording session for *The Wall* was as professional and thorough as any I'd ever seen. Any of the reported tension between the band members was not at all apparent while I was there. Dave and Roger knew exactly what they wanted for the album and worked with the zeal of artists who instinctively know they are creating a masterpiece. And although we didn't know it at the time, *The Wall* would go on to become one of the most imaginative and famous rock albums of all time, eventually spawning an animated "rock opera" feature-length musical film of the same name.

A few months after the album was released, I received a call at home from Dave Gilmour. He explained that Pink Floyd was planning to do a live performance of *The Wall* in five major cities around the world, kicking off at the Los Angeles Sports Arena. He first asked if I would be interested in touring with the band to sing backup for these five shows. It was a tempting thought because I knew the concerts were going to be magnificent theatrical productions attended by huge numbers of people, but I was busy doing Captain and Tennille projects so I politely declined the offer. However, I did accept Dave's invitation to attend the first concert in Los Angeles.

Daryl didn't want to go to the show, so I took Bruce Johnston's wife, Harriet, as my guest. Our seats were some of the best in the place, overlooking the huge stage where the band performed as a "wall" of huge faux stones was slowly built up between the band and the audience throughout the show. At the end, the wall was complete for a few moments, with the band completely hidden behind it, until the climax of the show brought it crashing down in a crescendo of sound. It was a thrilling and beautifully produced concert.

At one point a teenage boy sitting in front of us turned around and recognized me. A smirk appeared on his face. "What are *you* doing here?" he said, his voice dripping with disdain. Apparently my adult contemporary pop presence was ruining his adolescent rock fantasy.

I thought to myself, *Oh boy*, this *is going to be fun.*

"I'm here," I answered with a big, sweet smile, "as a guest of Dave Gilmour and Roger Waters. I sang backup vocals on *The Wall.*"

The kid narrowed his eyes. "You did *not!*"

"I most certainly did," I said, fully relishing the moment. "My name is on the album credits."

"Well," he said. "My friend brought one of the albums here to the show. I'm gonna go look myself." And with that he got up and squeezed his way down the aisle. Harriet and I exchanged knowing smiles.

When the kid returned a few minutes later, the contemptuous sneer on his face had been replaced by a look of awe. Almost shyly he held out his program to me. "Can I have your autograph?"

I confess that I reveled in the admiration of this young rock fan because for the moment, I, Toni Tennille, was actually . . . cool.

CHAPTER 17

ONE DAY IN LATE 1978 JERRY MOSS ASKED US TO MEET WITH him at his office at A&M.

Once we sat down Jerry got straight to the point. "We want our next Captain and Tennille release to be a greatest hits album!" he said enthusiastically.

Daryl and I knew right away what that meant: A&M didn't think we could produce any more hits. We felt otherwise, but Jerry was adamant. "We're going to do the greatest hits album," he said. And that was that. While Herb Alpert had always been the creative mind at A&M, Jerry was all business. He was determined to squeeze every last penny he could out of Captain and Tennille before, as we knew, we'd most likely be unceremoniously dropped from the label.

Around this time though, another record label, Casablanca, had been letting us know that they were interested in signing us. We were greatly chagrined that A&M had insisted on putting out the greatest hits album despite our objection, so the timing seemed right to start fresh with another label. The *Captain & Tennille Greatest Hits* album became the last we would release with A&M, and soon after we signed with Casablanca.

It's ironic that one of pop music's most "wholesome duos" would end up joining one of the decade's most notorious record labels. When we got on board, Casablanca was flying high on the success of such acts as the shock-rock group KISS as well as danceable hits from new stars emerging from the disco spectrum. Among these were the Village People and most notably Donna Summer, who was arguably the "Queen of Disco" and had scored numerous gold and platinum hits for the label. Adding Captain and Tennille to that motley roster was a little like trying to fit a square peg into a glitter-coated round hole, but the visionary young label head Neil Bogart saw that there was still potential for us to have another hit. Many of the Casablanca staff and executives were *also* flying high on something else, and I'm not talking about private planes.

Casablanca had a very talented promotion guy on its team who had been hugely successful doing promotions for Motown. This man was older than the rest of the staff, probably in his mid- to late forties, and Daryl and I liked him right away. Shortly after we'd joined the label, we had lunch with him to discuss promotion for our new album. Then to our surprise, he began to talk about the rampant drug use at the label.

"Now, I don't use drugs myself," he said, "and never have. But I think you guys need to understand exactly what is going on at Casablanca." He went on to explain that when the label had meetings, there would often be a pile of cocaine sitting right there in the middle of the conference table. As the staff discussed strategy and promotion schedules, they would lean over and take a snort from the pile.

The label's hard-partying antics have been the fodder of legend, the subject of numerous articles and a book, and even the basis of a possible television series. We never saw this firsthand—everyone knew to hide the drugs when Toni and Daryl were around—but it was common knowledge that Casablanca was the true "party" label. I have to admit, though, despite their unorthodox conferences and coffee breaks, the label—and especially Neil Bogart—really worked hard for us.

Once we'd gathered the songs we wanted to include on our first Casablanca release, *Make Your Move*, we invited Neil and some of the other label's executives over to listen to the selections that we had chosen so far. On the list was a song that I had written, titled "Do That to Me One More Time," which I sang for the group while playing the piano. I liked the song a lot, but I didn't think it had hit potential. But the moment that I finished, Bruce

Bird, Casablanca's big, jovial, vice president, jumped up out of his seat. "That's a smash!" he yelled. "Play it again!"

And Bruce was right. "Do That to Me One More Time," a sensual song of physical and emotional longing, which of course reflected my feelings for my distant husband, became Captain and Tennille's second number-one hit. And even sweeter was the knowledge that this song had been written by *me*, not someone else as many of our other hits had been. Its tremendous success cemented the confidence that I really *was* a songwriter, and that I could write songs with hit potential. But over the years, I'd always been hesitant to pitch my songs to other artists, even if I thought the songs would be perfect for them. My songs are so personal to me that the idea of rejection is just too painful, even though I know deep inside that many of my songs are really, *really* good.

Just as we were finishing up *Make Your Move*, I was approached by Bob Eubanks, the famous host of *The Newlywed Game* who was making quite a name for himself behind the camera producing television shows. He had been a fan of *The Captain and Tennille Show*, and he pitched the idea to me for a Toni Tennille syndicated talk/variety show. I was instantly intrigued.

Ever since watching my mother do her own talk show back in Montgomery, I'd always thought it would be fun to do a talk show of my own. As Bob and I envisioned it, *The Toni Tennille Show* would be part interviews with celebrity guests and lots of great music. We put a terrific band together for the show, including a fabulous sax, flute, and clarinet player named Rusty Higgins. Rusty had started touring with Captain and Tennille back in 1978 and later conducted for me beginning in 1984 during the years I sang the Great American Songbook with symphony orchestras and big bands.

With a change of set design, we turned what had been the studio where Dinah Shore had taped her talk show to *The Toni Tennille Show*. Dinah, who was one of the loveliest ladies I've ever met in show business, had ended her show shortly before I began taping mine. Daryl and I had been guests on Dinah's show several times, and I'd been delighted to find she had the kind of honest, down-to-earth personality that was so rare in the ego-driven world of show business. She and I had both been born and raised in the south—she was from Tennessee—so we got along beautifully.

When I walked into my dressing room on the very first day of taping my show, I found a huge arrangement of flowers with a lovely handwritten note of congratulations and good wishes from Dinah. The dressing room had been hers for years and was still decorated in her feminine, elegant style. I thought the dressing room was perfect and didn't change a thing!

The schedule for creating a five-day-per-week show is unrelenting. We taped a total of six shows in three days every week: five to air each week, and one to "put in the bank." Within that timeframe, I had to prepare for all the guests I'd be interviewing and rehearse the three or four songs that I would sing for each show. Doing the talk show was even harder than when I'd done *The Captain and Tennille Show*, but I loved it. And best of all I didn't have to pretend to dance!

I had a stellar crew who worked hard but still managed to have fun. I'll never forget our show conductor Ira Newborn. Ira, who stood maybe five feet six inches, is a brilliant guitarist and all-around fine musician. He is also a very funny man and cracked me up constantly. Ira liked to sidle up to me as I was taking my place behind the curtain waiting to make my entrance. I towered almost a foot above him in my four-inch heels. Ira would gaze up at me and, with his head tilted back, he would declare with a Romeo sigh, "Oh, Tonelda . . . *mein Valkyrie*. Be mine!" People associated with the show called me "Tonelda" for years after that, thanks to Ira.

I really loved doing my talk show because it gave me the opportunity to host some of my own favorite stars. Some of the standouts in my mind were Richard Chamberlain, a true gentleman in every sense of the word, and Charlton Heston, who exuded so much charisma that he nearly knocked me off my feet when I first met him. Another memorable guest was the ice skater Dorothy Hamill who, with her exuberant charm and gold medal performance at the 1976 Olympics, had cemented her place as "America's Sweetheart." We arranged to shoot at a local ice rink where Dorothy and I would perform a silly skit. I dressed up in a fur-trimmed hood and pretended to be the famous Norwegian Olympic figure skater and movie star Sonja Henie—except this "Sonja" didn't know how to skate. Dorothy patiently led me around the rink "teaching" Sonja the basics. Although I looked ridiculous wobbling around on my skates, things were going fine until I attempted a simple maneuver and landed flat on the ice, hurting my back. The director, of course, thought my fall was incredibly funny and kept it in the skit. But Dorothy was such a sweet and fun guest that my painful spill was worth having her on the show.

Of course not every guest was so lovely. I was initially very excited when the producers booked the actor Chevy Chase, who had just starred in the classic golf-comedy hit *Caddyshack*, which I loved. But Chevy ended up being one of the most difficult people I'd ever had to interview. He refused to be interviewed in front of the live audience, so we had to make arrangements to tape his interview separately. Then when Chevy arrived for the taping, he kept interrupting the interview to get up and leave the set. These abrupt "breaks" during the interview would bring the whole crew to a halt, and it threw me off the natural flow of conversation. Even worse, he wore a perpetual look of boredom on his face the whole time, responding to my questions with short, sarcastic answers.

There have been times that I too had to sit down to an interview when I really didn't feel like it, but I have always believed that people should be treated with respect no matter what the situation—especially when you are a guest on their television show!

We were all very grateful when Chevy's taping was finished and he promptly left.

Later, a rumor surfaced that Chevy had "reduced me to tears" on the show by his rudeness. I was so insulted by his rude behavior that I likely did shed some tears of anger and frustration after I got back to the privacy of my dressing room. But the whole time we were taping, I remained as stoic and gracious as I could. Damned if I was ever going to allow *anyone* to make me break down on my own show!

Another person who proved to be a difficult guest on the show was my own husband. The producers were always asking me to have Daryl come on the show so I could interview him. He had already been on several times as a musical guest but hadn't done any talking in front of the camera. In spite of my misgivings, I reluctantly agreed. I'd been enjoying the freedom of working without Daryl's tight grip and unpredictable moods, so having him on the show to interview reminded me how nervous he'd made me feel when we were doing *The Captain and Tennille Show*. We performed a couple of songs together once the crew had assembled the mountain of keyboards and synthesizers he'd brought. That was the easy part. But then I had to sit down and try to get through the painful process of *interviewing* Daryl. He would respond to my questions with odd, vague answers that seemed to come out of nowhere and often had *nothing* to do with what I'd asked him. It was as though he enjoyed watching me squirm as I tried to interpret whatever weird thing he'd just said into some kind of "normal" banter that the audience could understand. I think a clip of that interview is available online, but I refuse to watch it because it takes me right back to my painful struggle over the years to understand Daryl.

Despite all the heart and love that went into making *The Toni Tennille Show*, syndicated television can be a crapshoot. Some television stations played the show at good viewing times but others did not, so we never got the consistent ratings needed to attract sponsors. We closed the show after one year. But I'd already noticed that talk shows were starting to change, and it was in a direction I didn't feel comfortable with. For one of the last episodes, the producers had talked me into reuniting a pair of adopted adult siblings with their long-lost birth mother—right there on my show. This was a completely contrived setup, and I was uncomfortable with the inclusion of a television audience in what should have been a private event.

Reality television was not yet hugely popular, but even then audiences were starting to develop voyeuristic appetites. People were beginning to lose interest in music on daytime TV; that was what MTV and music videos were for. The sensationalism of "real" people's lives eventually took over talk shows and spawned the reality TV genre that dominates media to this day.

I didn't have much free time to mourn the ending of *The Toni Tennille Show*. It was time to make our second Captain and Tennille album for Casablanca that we titled *Keeping Our Love Warm*. For the cover Daryl and I were photographed on a set that had been built inside the photographer's studio to resemble a steam room. Wrapped only in skimpy towels as we reclined among billowing clouds of simulated steam, Daryl wore his white captain's hat and I had my damp hair slicked back from my face. And just like on the *Dream* cover, my short pink towel revealed quite a bit of my tanned thighs, courtesy of a thick coat of bronzer applied by the makeup artist.

The album title came from a song I wrote, again with Daryl in mind, about a woman who has to spend time away but wants to assure her lover that she is:

> Keeping our love warm, keeping myself on cool,
> Keeping our love warm, living by the lover's rule.

As a nod to Casablanca's disco-fueled reputation, Daryl and I tried our hand at disco with a song that I had written called

"How Can You Be So Cold?" Of course, the song was again about my relationship with Daryl:

> How can you be so cold . . . when I'm so hot?
> How can you be so distant and cool,
> When I am not?
> I'm on fire and I'm burning, burning, burning with desire . . .

If Daryl ever wondered where I was getting the inspiration for my lyrics, he never once asked.

But not every song I wrote was about Daryl. "Don't Forget Me" is among the songs that I am proudest of both lyrically and musically. It was inspired by the movie *Kramer vs. Kramer* that starred Meryl Streep and Dustin Hoffman who play two people who love one another but just simply cannot live together.

Another song I wrote for *Keeping Our Love Warm* was "Gentle Stranger"—and this one was definitely *not* about Daryl. It told the story of a handsome young man I'd met on the beach at Malibu shortly before I had begun a relationship with Daryl. Daryl had been off on tour with the Beach Boys and I was back in LA, lonely, adrift, and trying to figure out where my life was going. After spending the day together strolling the beach and lying in the sun, this young man and I had a passionate and beautiful one-night love affair:

> Gentle stranger, you came into my life when I was feeling sad
> And I looked up one day to see your face shining in the sun.
> Your eyes were kind and you spoke softly to me

The song ends with this refrain:

> I am warm, I am safe from harm, I am loved.
> I am loved, I am loved,
> I am loved.

Imagine my surprise when we began to get mail from fans who had interpreted this song in a very different way: They thought I had written it about Jesus! Although my inspiration had been something very different, the song captures the warmth and comfort of feeling loved. Whether it is heavenly love or the romantic kind can be left entirely up to the listener to decide.

Keeping Our Love Warm, released in 1980, didn't produce the smash hit that *Make Your Move* had, but it sold well. By that time the Casablanca label was beginning to show signs of stress, which was undoubtedly not helped by the overspending, careless accounting, and personal indulgences of its staff. Neil Bogart, who had already left Casablanca, died of cancer at the tragically young age of 39. The label was eventually absorbed by Polygram Records. Neil had been the true spirit of the label; through his instincts and chutzpah, Casablanca had risen from an insignificant little company into a label that had literally gazed into the crystal ball of music trends, many of which still echo in twenty-first-century popular music.

Daryl and I realized that *Keeping Our Love Warm* would be our last Captain and Tennille album. Polygram was busy ripping the remnants of Casablanca apart and had very little interest in us. We had both tired of living in the glittery chaos of Los Angeles and decided to sell our Pacific Palisades home. As it was in one of the most private and desirable areas of LA, a lot of celebrities and music people came through to view it, including Bob Dylan. Our listing agent reported that Bob had walked glumly through the house and afterward opined curtly, "Too many goddamned flowers." Apparently he did not appreciate my decorating style at the time; there was French floral wallpaper of a different color in every room. We eventually sold the house to Steven Bochco, the creator of the breakout television show *Hill Street Blues*.

Our next home was over four hundred miles away from Los Angeles in the majestic Sierra Nevada range at Lake Tahoe, whose cold and impossibly crystal clear waters straddled the

Nevada-California border. Our property, a beautiful, gently slop-
ing lot that looked across a wide meadow, was nestled among
pine trees on the eastern shore of the lake in the Glenbrook community. Daryl had decided we should build a real log cabin, and
I thought it sounded like a fun idea so I went along with it. He
obsessed over house plans with the architect we'd hired, constantly making changes and additions. I soon came to realize that
building a log cabin house—the way Daryl envisioned it—is not
nearly as easy as you might think.

All of the enormous logs that formed both the interior and
exterior of the house were harvested from a forest in Idaho where
they had been standing dead for many years. Each log was then
transported, one by one, via helicopter to a mill where they were
carefully trimmed down to size before being trucked to our construction site in Nevada.

We began construction in the fall of 1982, the year that
proved to be one of the worst, snowiest winters that Tahoe ever
had. Consequently, it took two years to build our Tahoe home.
When it was finally complete our log "cabin" was more like a log
"lodge," a huge four-story house with enough room for ten people. It had fireplaces so big you could practically walk into them!
And of course, it had cost a fortune to build. Although I couldn't
understand why we had to have such an enormous home, Daryl
had insisted we needed the space. I had to admit the finished
house was absolutely beautiful inside and out.

Even after all the time and trouble it took to build the house,
we didn't get to spend as much time in it as I would have liked,
because we were often on tour. And even though Daryl had
included an excellent home recording studio in our Tahoe home,
he had always wanted to own a real professional studio. He built a
state-of-the-art recording studio in the San Fernando Valley and
named it Rumbo Recorders after a beloved stuffed elephant he'd
had as a child. Daryl's long-time dream of owning a renowned
studio came to fruition as a diverse roster of famous artists came

to record there: Guns N' Roses, Bob Seger, Joe Cocker, Megadeth, the Traveling Wilburys, and Barry Manilow, among many others.

We were also still busy performing as Captain and Tennille at various venues around the country and doing week-long gigs in Las Vegas. It was during one of these Las Vegas engagements that out of the blue, Daryl decided to fire all of our backup singers—including my sister Louisa.

Melissa, who had been a regular part of our television show and sang on many of our albums, had toured with Captain and Tennille for three years before leaving to start a family with her husband, Andy. While raising her family in southern California, she occasionally acted in some television commercials and remained active in local singing groups and choirs. Even Carmen Dragon, Daryl's notoriously discerning father, was so captivated by Melissa's glorious lyric soprano voice that he asked her to sing as a guest artist in the very last concert he conducted with the Redlands Symphony in 1983. Later Melissa went on to become a behavioral analysis interventionist (BAI), working with autistic children and, in her free time, conducting children's choirs.

Louisa toured with Captain and Tennille for seven years and was still with us when we were performing our Las Vegas shows. As usual, Daryl didn't consult me before he abruptly announced his decision to the singers one evening in between Vegas shows. He'd figured it would be more cost effective to just have our musicians double as backup singers. Louisa came to me in tears. She was hurt at the callous and sudden way Daryl had dismissed her and the other singers, and she was especially upset that she wouldn't be joining us on our upcoming tour to Australia. I went to Daryl and insisted that the singers be able to at least come with us to Australia. He reluctantly agreed.

After we got back from Australia, Louisa left the music business and began her long career as a schoolteacher. I could not have been more proud of her; she was a wonderful teacher and loved her new role. Still, I missed her terribly and was sad how things had ended. But Daryl was determined to have complete control over everything in our lives, and I felt helpless to intervene.

Once again, I could feel myself chafing at the bit to get away from Daryl's autocratic grip and the consequential anxiety and stress it created. Now that we had decided to cut Captain and Tennille back to only a few performances a year, I thought it was a good time for me to pursue another dream: to sing the songs of the great American songbook with symphony orchestras and big bands. Ever since I was a little girl and Daddy had sat me and my sisters down in front of the hi-fi with a stack of records, I'd adored singing the romantic, swinging, and sophisticated songs of the first half of the twentieth century. I thought that perhaps I could get some bookings with orchestras around the country as a solo singer. Daryl was fine with my going on the road without him. He also liked the idea of my bringing in some steady income since we weren't doing that many Captain and Tennille gigs.

Just as Daddy had done for me and my sisters, I wanted to make my program of standards a kind of storybook for the listener, many of whom I figured might not be very familiar with the genre. I would talk a little about the composers and tell stories about them that I had heard from Daddy or had discovered from my own research.

And so began the most joyous and fulfilling years of my entire career.

CHAPTER 18

Although I've always cherished and appreciated the experience of performing and recording as Captain and Tennille, there has always been a special place in my heart for the classic songs of the 1920s, '30s, and '40s—the songs Daddy loved so much. Now that Daryl and I had set Captain and Tennille aside, save for a few performances a year, I finally had the chance to do something I had always wanted to do: sing the great American songbook with symphony orchestras.

I wanted to have a theme for my concerts, so I created my first symphony program around some of my favorite songs by the great composers George Gershwin, Jerome Kern, and Irving Berlin. I hired Sammy Nestico, a composer and arranger of great renown, to write the arrangements. Born in 1924, Sammy was, and as I write this still is, a brilliant musician and a legendary arranger. Throughout his long and illustrious career, he has arranged for many of the greats, including Sarah Vaughn and the Count Basie Orchestra.

I'd first met Sammy when he had been hired to write arrangements for me for *The Captain and Tennille Show*. Just like me, Sammy believes that the lyrics of a song are just as important as the notes, so he pays equal attention to both, and is very careful to not let the arrangement overpower or get in the way of the voice. Instead he uses the instruments to "comment on" and highlight the words. In addition to being an incredible talent, Sammy is also a sweet, dear, and loving person. Sammy and I have always said that we were "joined at the heart," and every moment I spent working with him was a joyful highlight of my musical life.

Symphony arrangements are very expensive to create, and you have to have parts made for at least eighty musicians. At the time I had no idea if I could get enough bookings to justify the large expense, but I decided to take the gamble and hope that the investment would pay off. Once I had chosen all the songs and Sammy had written the arrangements, it was time to try them out in front of a real live audience. We chose a regional orchestra in a midsize town in Colorado to have a run-though and rehearsal of the music, after which I would perform it in concert for a local audience. Now, regional orchestras are often made up of part-time musicians, most of whom have regular day jobs but play music in their spare time. While a lot of these musicians are incredibly talented, as a group the quality of regional orchestras usually can't come close to a true professional one. Knowing this, Sammy asked if I wanted him to simplify the charts to make them easier for a less-skilled regional orchestra to play. No, I said. I wanted him to write the parts as he would for the finest orchestral musicians in the world. Having studied classical piano for so long myself I understood how hard these musicians had practiced to perfect their skills, and I wanted to make sure the parts were challenging and interesting, not just a bunch of whole notes. We'd have to take our chances at the run-through and hope for the best.

Sammy didn't hold back one bit. As a result the complex charts were a little tough for the regional orchestra to play and rehearsal was a pretty long affair. But I was able to hear immediately that the orchestrations, although challenging, were absolutely brilliant. And despite the slips here and there from the orchestra, the musicians played with enthusiasm, and the audience seemed to love the concert. Soon I began to get bookings all over the US and even in Canada with fine orchestras in Pittsburgh, Cincinnati, Atlanta, St. Louis, Edmonton, and many more.

I can't begin to explain how humbled and thrilled I was to appear with these orchestras. I would stand in the wings listening to the first burst of applause as the concertmaster entered and took his bow before signaling the musicians to tune to the oboe's A. Once my conductor Rusty Higgins took the stage and led the orchestra in the introduction to my first song, I would make my entrance in a long, lovely gown feeling like Cinderella at the ball. And luckily my audiences throughout those years came to enjoy the songs as much as I did.

When I began touring solo in 1984, Daryl and I were living in Lake Tahoe and the closest airport was in Reno, a couple hours' drive away. Whenever I headed out for a concert, I made the long drive back and forth by myself, usually three or four times a month. One winter I flew home from a concert and arrived in Reno late in the afternoon. After I had retrieved my luggage and located my car in the parking garage, I began the long drive home that would take me up over Spooner Summit to Lake Tahoe. I noticed that the sky was darkening quickly and the snow, which had just been coming down in light flurries when I'd left the airport, had now begun to descend in thick curtains, making it hard for me to see out of the windshield. It was too late to turn back, so I gripped the wheel and navigated slowly and carefully through the Washoe Valley to Carson City, before turning onto steep, winding Highway 50 and continuing up to seven-thousand-foot Spooner Summit. Only after cresting the summit would I finally be just a few miles from home.

When I tapped the brakes I could feel the tires slipping a bit on the road, which had frozen into a slick layer of black ice under the buildup of snow. It was quite dark by this time and I was terrified that I might misjudge a curve in the road and careen off the mountain. On the radio, a commentator from the local weather station warned that people should keep off the roads until the snowstorm passed. This didn't help me one bit since I was now deep into the mountains and had no choice but to continue on toward home. With my concentration already worn thin from the long flight, it took every ounce of adrenaline to keep focused on the road as the snowfall became heavier. Thankfully I made it home alive.

The next morning I said to Daryl "I just can't take this interminable drive to the airport any more ... especially in the winter."

We hadn't learned until after moving into our log house that the snow levels in the Tahoe mountains could be enormous. And since most of the people who had homes in our community lived there only during the summer, the streets were only sporadically plowed in the winter. Sometimes I had to shovel for three hours just to be able to pull my car out of the garage and the snow-covered driveway!

We decided to build a new house on five acres down in Washoe Valley, about an hour east of Lake Tahoe. The site sat at an elevation of five thousand feet with a sweeping view of the beautiful valley dotted with old apple orchards and towering pines. There were magnificent views of the Sierra foothills to the west and the same crisp, clean mountain air we'd so loved in Lake Tahoe. At night, the coyote's eerie and mournful voices drifted along the wind from deep in the hills. It was a peaceful and beautiful place to make a new home. *And* it was only a half an hour from the airport.

Daryl, who had laid out the design of our log cabin, immediately got to work drawing out the plans for our new home. He had a genuine, though unschooled, gift for architecture and home design. "Why don't we make this next house a little *smaller?*" was my only suggestion. The log house had been way too large for just the two of us, with many of the rooms remaining practically unused. And, I added gently, building a smaller house would also save us some money. But Daryl had already decided on the plans for the new house and there would be no stopping him once he got started.

When it was done, the Washoe Valley house was almost as large as the house in Lake Tahoe—and this time Daryl had included a separate guesthouse. We had acquired so much stuff—all kinds of musical instruments and recording equipment, computers, boxes of sheet music—that all of it wouldn't fit into our new house despite its size, so Daryl rented a huge warehouse in Carson City to hold the items he couldn't bear to part with, and there they remained until we moved from Washoe Valley years later.

Even though we had retired Captain and Tennille, I was making a good income with my symphony tours. So, as usual Daryl ignored my suggestions of a smaller, cozier house. He built the house he wanted, paying little attention to the money spent.

Our hopes for less snow were dashed when we spent our first winter in the new house. Even though we were one thousand feet lower in elevation than we had been in Lake Tahoe, winters in Washoe Valley were almost as grueling. I'd have to dig out a channel in sometimes shoulder-high snow from the dog door to the backyard so our dogs could get out to relieve themselves! At least the main roads in our new community were plowed all through the winter so I could drive back and forth to the airport without worrying that I'd go off the side of a mountain. And because I was starting to get a lot of bookings to play with symphonies and big bands around the country, I had to make the trip several times a month.

Orchestras understand that performing "pops" with guest artists is part of the job, even if many of the classically trained musicians didn't particularly enjoy doing it. Concerts featuring pop artists are very popular with audiences and often bring in a large amount of income through ticket sales. So including this "lighter fare" in the season, along with concerts featuring classical music, is important for the orchestra's budget.

I don't blame many of these musicians for their hesitation. I'd heard stories about guest artists who'd arrived for rehearsal late and unprepared, while at the same time presenting a detailed list of diva-type demands for specific foods or wines in their dressing rooms. I was determined to show respect to each of the orchestras I played with and to prove that I was not *that* kind of diva. I always arrived neatly dressed and ready to work—not fresh off the plane in my sweatpants, as other guests had—and I insisted that the musicians I brought with me do the same. What always made me happiest was when musicians would approach me after a concert to tell me how much they had enjoyed playing my arrangements. The arrangements that Sammy had created were fun and challenging even for the most accomplished musicians, and they appreciated it.

So many of the classic songs I sang with the symphonies made me think about my father. Daddy and I had kept a kind of wary truce in the years since he and Mother had divorced. He'd quickly remarried, but his second wife had never warmed to the idea that Daddy had four daughters whom he loved, and she resented any time or attention that he gave to us. So even though Daddy lived in Orange County, only about an hour away from Los Angeles where Daryl and I had lived for many years, I only saw him on rare occasions.

Daddy's life had changed a lot in the latter years of his life. He finally got sober; he never drank again. And he started working as a salesman for EZ Go golf carts, a job that he both loved and excelled at. Daddy's charisma, love of the sport, and ability to make instant friends with virtually anyone made him a natural for sales. Although I was happy that he was now living what appeared to be a stable life, our relationship had drifted over the years. I would see Daddy at Christmas or some other holiday, and he would occasionally come to some of our shows, but our time together was short and, quite honestly, uncomfortable for me. My own life had been nonstop and hectic for a decade, with touring, making records, and doing television shows, which allowed me to keep a distance from Daddy. And at the same time, it was also an excuse for me to ignore the painful memories that I associated with him.

While Daddy had been very proud of my success with Captain and Tennille—he loved seeing the Tennille name "up in lights" so to speak—he was absolutely overcome with pride and joy when I started my solo career singing the standards. This was the same music Daddy had loved his whole life; it was the sound that had bewitched him as a young man and had never let go, even when he'd had to abandon his exciting career as a singer.

The standards were the songs that Daddy shared with me when I was a girl. He would twirl his finger to demonstrate the genius lilt of Gershwin's piano or punch a fist in the air just at the moment of a glorious climax of horns and drums in Tommy Dorsey's orchestra. The witty, poetic, and carefully-crafted lyrics of that era moved Daddy so much as he sang along to recordings of Frank Sinatra or Tony Bennett. As I stood onstage singing those same songs, the good memories of Daddy slowly transcended the bad. His genes had helped make me who I was and, and even more important, it had been his love of music that had nurtured mine.

I remember when Daddy came up to Los Angeles in 1984 to watch the recording session for my first album of standards, *More Than You Know*. Sammy Nestico arranged the songs and conducted the orchestra of top musicians for the session. I sang every song live with the orchestra, just as Sinatra used to do. I'll never forget standing in the control room, behind Daddy and Sammy, those two unabashedly romantic men, as they listened to a playback of the beautiful Gershwin tune "Our Love Is Here to Stay." As Sammy's gorgeous orchestration and my voice filled the small room, tears slipped from the eyes of both men. And then I felt my own tears as I watched them.

One night a few years later, just before I was about to leave for a symphony gig out of town, Daddy called. "I feel something down in my throat when I swallow," he said after we'd chatted for a few minutes. "But I'm getting it checked out with the doctor later this week."

Daddy was trying to be nonchalant, but I knew immediately that this was something serious. Not only had he been a binge-drinking alcoholic for so many years of his life, he'd also been a three-pack-a-day smoker since the age of fourteen until finally quitting in his early seventies. As I drove to the airport the next morning, I couldn't shake the feeling that Daddy might be very ill. And he was. The doctor diagnosed him with esophageal cancer.

I asked a gastroenterologist friend about how serious this kind of cancer was, and he looked at me sadly. "Toni," he said, "I'm going to be honest with you. Esophageal cancer is what is known as the 'smoker and drinker's' cancer. The prognosis from diagnosis to death is usually about six months."

The news hit me hard and only confirmed what I had feared. Once I'd absorbed the news and accepted it, I made the decision to make the most of the little time I had left with my father. In the past Daddy's outpouring of emotion had usually repelled me—because it usually happened when he was drunk. Now his tears came from joy and love, not shame and regret. I have always been grateful that I had that special time with Daddy, when he could be a part of something that was so important to both of us.

A few months after Daddy's diagnosis, I received a call that he was under hospice care at his home and had only a short time to live. I left immediately to be by his side with Louisa while we waited for Jane and Melissa to arrive. Daddy was in and out of consciousness and at times hallucinating, but Louisa and I held his hand and talked to him. We weren't sure if he could hear us, but still we talked for hours about the great times we'd had back in Alabama—swimming at the lake, posing for Daddy's ever-present camera, and of course, making music. He was ghastly thin, being fed by a feeding tube inserted in his stomach, and it was horrible to see him that way. But I think it was a comfort to know that two of his four beloved daughters were there with him.

Later that night as Daddy lay sleeping, I left to catch a few hours of sleep at my hotel with plans to return early the next morning. At 4 a.m. Louisa called and told me to come back to the house—Daddy had died. The people from the funeral home were removing his body just as I arrived, and his face was uncovered as they wheeled him out of the room. I have tried ever since to remove from my mind that final image of my once-vibrant father now reduced to skin and bones, a mask of enduring pain frozen on his face. But I was grateful that I had managed to do what I should have done many years before and forgive him for the pain that his drinking had caused my mother and all my sisters. But I was also thankful that I had managed to forgive *myself* for all the anger that I'd harbored against him over the years.

After Daddy died, I often ended my live performances with Daddy's favorite song, "Tenderly," and I always dedicated it to him. After all, this was the same man who had insisted that when I'd severed my finger as a child I receive the best medical care possible, even if it cost more than my family could afford. If my father hadn't paid for the extensive surgeries that reconstructed my finger and enabled me to play piano and pursue music, my life would have been very different.

For thirty years Mother had been living in a small apartment in Newport Beach where she'd begun a career selling real estate after she and Daddy had divorced. She never remarried. Although she was living an active and independent life, I could see that she was beginning to slow down. Due to her diabetes which Mother, who loved sweets, didn't control as well as she should have her eyesight was failing quickly. So Daryl and I bought her a small house in Reno where she could still have her independence, which Mother fiercely treasured, and still be close to me.

Mother loved living in Reno and we saw each other, or at least talked on the phone, almost every day. My dear friend Dotty Lienau took Mother under her wing and the two became fast friends, which was a relief since I was still traveling quite a bit. It seemed I was always changing planes in Dallas, and I would call to check on Mother between flights. She would always answer the phone with the same question: "Toni, where are you?"

I would answer with a laugh, "I'm at the airport in Dallas, Mother." We had this same exchange so many times it became an inside joke between the two of us. Finally, one day when I once again called her from the Dallas airport, Mother laughed and said, "Toni, when you die, you're going to go through Dallas!"

CHAPTER 19

I ACTED IN MY VERY FIRST PLAY IN THE NINTH GRADE. THE production was *Father Knows Best*, and because I was easily the tallest girl in my class, I was cast in the role of Mother. After that I was hooked, and I continued to act whenever I could, playing everyone from Auntie Mame, to the princess in *Once Upon a Mattress*, to Lizzie in *The Rainmaker*.

Because I had a strong singing voice and could read music, I was often cast as the lead in musicals. My three sisters also liked to sing, so while we were growing up we'd break into spontaneous a cappella versions of songs from *South Pacific*, *Oklahoma*, and *Porgy and Bess*, where I always sang the baritone Porgy parts to Jane or Louisa's high, sweet Bess. We liked to do this on long rides in the car and sometimes sang the entire score to a musical at the top of our lungs—which drove Mother and Daddy crazy.

After moving to California I'd found a home again on the stage in productions at the Southcoast Repertory Theater, which led to the creation and production of the only musical I ever wrote, *Mother Earth*. The desire to fulfill my lifelong dream of performing on Broadway—that most magnificent of all stages— was still unrealized. But in early 1997 an opportunity arose that perhaps would allow me to fulfill that wish.

Julie Andrews had been starring in the Broadway production of the gender-bending musical *Victor/Victoria* since 1995. She had first played the lead role in the 1983 movie version that was written and directed by her husband, the renowned director Blake Edwards. The story, set in Paris during the Gay Thirties, is about Victoria Grant, a penniless woman who pretends to be a man in order to get a job performing as a drag queen. Along the way, Victoria falls in love with a real man who has no idea that she is a real woman and all kinds of ruckus ensues until she finally reveals her true self and the two live happily ever after. *Victor/Victoria's* delightful score was one of the last written by the beloved and prolific composer Henry Mancini. When Henry passed away in 1994 from pancreatic cancer, the score was completed by Frank Wildhorn. The show was a Broadway smash, with Julie carrying the weight of it on her slender shoulders and crystalline voice. Two nonstop years later she was understandably exhausted. I'd heard through the grapevine that Julie had wanted to quit for quite a while but felt obligated to continue since the show was so profitable. Eventually all that relentless singing left nodes on her vocal cords, which is every singer's worst nightmare. There was no way she could go on. After making a farewell appearance to a roaring standing ovation, Julie quit the show and retired from the stage.

Once Julie decided to leave the production, the search immediately went out for her replacement. When a friend in the business suggested that I look into auditioning for the role, I realized that fate was unlocking a door for me. I was confident that I could act the part, and my tall, small-busted build would allow me to easily portray a man onstage. *I can do this!* I thought. The possibility of finally playing in a Broadway musical—something that so many actors can only dream of—made me giddy. And I was more than ready for a new challenge.

I thought about Julie's vocal problems during *Victor/Victoria* as I began studying the score. I had been concerned that all the songs would be written in a key suitable for a soprano. I am definitely a tenor and tend to sing in my "chest voice." But as I began to sing through the songs, I realized they were very comfortable for my range and that they would have been hard for Julie, a lyric soprano. I wondered if singing night after night in an uncomfortable range could have contributed to the problems with her vocal cords. The only problem I had with the score was one high note— so high it would literally shatter glass—that my character would sing a few times in the show. When I was feeling 100 percent I could fake a pretty good mezzo-soprano high note, but if I was in the least compromised by a cold or allergies it was impossible. The director and I decided to pre-record the high note in case I was having trouble with my voice and then I could pantomime it onstage.

Quickly I put together an audition tape of me acting and singing a few key scenes from the show. It was professionally produced and very expensive to make, but the end results were really good, and I felt sure it would help me win the coveted role. But no sooner had I sent off the video than I learned that Raquel Welch had been cast in the role of Victoria. I was too late. And being the self-deprecating type that I am, I scolded myself for thinking I'd even *had* a chance. After all, Raquel had already starred in a Broadway musical; I had only acted in regional theater and on television shows. Still, I had a hard time imagining that the very busty Raquel, who stood at most five feet four inches tall, could convincingly play the role of a man.

Apparently, neither could the audiences. A few weeks after Julie left the show and Raquel took over the part *Victor/Victoria* closed on Broadway. The show just couldn't make it without Julie. It might not have made it much longer if I had been in the role, but I sure would have liked a chance to try.

Not long after, the announcement came that *Victor/Victoria* would close on Broadway and embark on a national tour. The producers and director had watched my audition video and offered me the role for the tour. I was torn: If I had been able to do the show on Broadway, Daryl and I could have rented an apartment in New York and moved our dogs and cats there while the production ran. Getting a chance to live in New York City for a while might have been a fun adventure. Going on the road with the show was an entirely different story. But still, I *really* wanted the part.

At the time I didn't know much about how touring theater productions worked. Rather naïvely, I thought the show would play in larger cities like Toronto and Chicago for a couple of months at a time before moving on to the next place. Daryl and the pets could come with me to each place, and we could rent an apartment as our home base. There would still be a semblance of a normal life, even if I was performing eight shows a week.

Looking back, I realize I should have insisted that the producers give me a more concrete explanation of the show's schedule before I agreed to sign on. But again, I wanted that part so badly I could taste it, and I just knew I'd be good at it. By now things were moving at warp-speed; I needed to make a decision or I'd lose the role again. I signed the contract.

It wasn't until I flew out to New York to meet the show's producers and representatives from the tour company that I learned all my assumptions had been wrong. The travel schedule for *Victor/Victoria* would include a month of rehearsals in New York City and then forty weeks on the road, changing cities every week and, sometimes, even stopping in two different cities in a single week. In addition to the eight shows a week that I would perform as the lead role, I was also required to do television interviews the opening day in each new city and phone interviews throughout the rest of the week to promote the show for the next stop.

As the ramifications of the commitment that I had made sank in, I couldn't help but think back over the past few weeks leading up to my decision to sign on. Deep inside of me there had been a flicker of a feeling that something wasn't right, but in my eagerness to get the role I had ignored the warning signs. It was a classic mistake—one I had made before. And although I didn't realize it at the time, it was one that I would pay a huge price for. But the contract had been signed, and there was no going back.

Come on, Toni, I thought, trying to rally myself. *You're a big girl.* I had toured extensively with Captain and Tennille for years, and at the age of fifty-seven I was in the best health I'd been in my life. Years of singing with big bands and symphonies had kept my voice strong and flexible. If anyone could do this, I could.

Shrugging off my concern, I smiled and kept my misgivings to myself.

Once I got back to Nevada, Daryl and I sat down to figure out how we would handle the year that I would be away from home. The idea we'd originally had of renting places where our pets could stay with us was now out. Although he wasn't working or traveling at the time, Daryl refused to care for our pets by himself while I was gone—the responsibility of walking our two dogs and feeding them and our two cats was too much for him to handle. I enlisted Jennifer Dory, our longtime pet sitter and close friend, who agreed to move into our house and be a full-time caretaker for the animals while I was away. Daryl would move into the guesthouse, which was his decision, so that Jennifer could have the main house to herself while caring for the pets.

Knowing I would really need a personal assistant to travel with me and help me manage my time and activities, I hired Becky Greenlaw, who had worked with me as an assistant and road manager during the later years of Captain and Tennille and my solo career. Fortunately, I was able to convince Becky to come out of retirement and join me on the tour because she is exactly the kind of person you want with you: whip-smart, organized, and cool-headed. Becky, who'd had a long career as a producer and director for the daytime soap *Days of Our Lives* before she retired from the business, knew how to handle any situation no matter how crazy or unexpected.

We decided that Daryl would fly out every two weeks or so to whatever city I was in so we could spend some time together. With the domestic details settled—or so I thought—I began preparations to join the show for a year on the road.

Before I left for rehearsals in New York in August 1998, my sister Jane flew out from her home in Florida for a visit. For many years Jane and I had lived almost three thousand miles apart, but we share an almost telepathic kind of bond and instinctively know when something is wrong with the other. Although I was

extremely excited about the upcoming challenge, I was also having bouts of anxiety and had trouble sleeping. Jane said nothing at
the time of her visit and chalked it up to just anticipatory nerves
about having to leave home. But later she told me that she had
sensed I might be falling into a depression.

We flew to New York for a month of rehearsals before *Victor/
Victoria* hit the road. Becky had found the two of us a comfortable apartment-type hotel close to the rehearsal space, with an
extra room in my suite so Daryl could have his own space when
he came to visit. I was relieved to discover that the show's director, Mark Hoebee, was a wonderful guy whom I felt comfortable
with right away. He understood that I needed to make the role
of Victoria my own and, with the blessing of Blake Edwards and
the other producers, allowed me to drop the English accent and
use my own southern voice for the character. Not only was I concerned that my English accent wasn't perfect, but I also felt that
audiences strongly associated Victoria's English accent with Julie.

Before the producers and director had officially chosen me
for the role, Becky and I flew to New York to meet with them one
more time. It was a wonderful trip and I felt strong, confident,
and ready to make my mark. While we were there we attended a
performance of *Victor/Victoria* and got to see Julie in one of her
last appearances. I was especially excited because I would get to
meet her after the show. The moment she made her entrance on
the stage, the audience erupted in adoring applause. Julie's innate
beauty and charm radiated from the stage, and even though, as a
singer myself, I could tell she was struggling with her voice, the
audience was oblivious to any vocal problems she was having. Or
even if they did notice, they didn't care. She was truly mesmer-
izing, and her entire performance was wonderful.

After the show I was escorted back to Julie's dressing room.
When I first arrived, Julie was in an adjacent room changing
clothes, but her husband Blake Edwards was there, and he chatted
amiably with me while we waited. Blake was a fascinating man

who had directed some of the most legendary films in cinema history, including *The Pink Panther* movies and *Breakfast at Tiffany's*, and I was completely in awe of him. But he was so friendly and animated that I felt as if we had known each other for years. By the time we were finished speaking, he'd offered Daryl and me use of his and Julie's home in Switzerland anytime we wished! Of course, I knew Blake was just being kind in making such a generous offer to someone he'd just met, but it just shows the type of affable person he was.

Julie came in and greeted me warmly with a big hug. "I knew you were in the audience," she said with her lovely British accent. "I could hear you laugh!" Julie wished me well on my journey to pick up the role of Victoria where she had left off, and her enthusiastic blessing buoyed my spirits. Getting to meet her was one of my fondest memories of *Victor/Victoria*. Many of the memories to come were not so delightful.

During the month that we were in New York for rehearsals, I got to know the cast and crew of the show and found them all to be wonderful, hard-working people. Most were thrilled to be doing the thing they loved best and were grateful for the opportunity to earn a living while doing it. Being around these young people, who would be my family for the next year and who were so excited at the idea of having a yearlong paying gig, made me feel a little guilty about how much I worried about the upcoming tour.

After rehearsals we moved the entire production to Reno, Nevada, for final technical run-throughs, which meant we spent most of the day "blocking" and methodically rehearsing the show before doing a performance later that same night for a live audience. I was only a short distance from home, performing in the same theater where I had guest starred with the Reno Philharmonic Orchestra many times, and it made me feel homesick even before we'd actually started the tour.

It was at this time that I realized just how demanding the role of Victoria was—she is onstage from five minutes after the curtain goes up until the very end, with just one three-minute break while another character sings a solo. Victoria sings about eleven songs and has numerous costume changes that must be done in seconds before the next scene starts. And the set is two-story, so the cast spends a lot of the show racing up and down stairs. And then there is the dancing . . . Oh boy.

I thought I'd seen the last of dancing when we ended *The Captain and Tennille Show,* but I was sadly mistaken. *Victor/Victoria* is riddled with dance numbers and once again I found myself in the uncomfortable position of trying to pull off respectable moves among a cast of professional dancers. But the choreographer gave me steps I felt comfortable with and the rest of the show's fabulous dancers made me look pretty good.

This all might have been fine if the production had been in one place, but being on the road left no time to recuperate between cities and shows. We kicked off the national tour of *Victor/Victoria* in Portland, Oregon, in September. Portland was warm and beautiful and we got some great initial reviews for the production. I took a deep breath and dove in.

As the tour made its way from one city to the next, the weeks began to unroll into a blur of routine. Mondays were travel days. Tuesdays were for interviews with local television and radio, followed by a run-through of the show after the set was up in the new venue. Later that same evening we would have the opening-night performance, which was always nerve-wracking because that is the show that the theater critics attend. There were nightly shows Wednesday, Thursday, and Friday, with phone interviews in between. Then came the weekend: there were two shows each on both Saturdays and Sundays, a matinee at 3 p.m. and then an evening show at the regular time. The moment the curtain came down after the last Sunday show, the crew would swarm over the stage to start breaking it down for transport to the next city.

Becky proved to be a steady and comforting presence, always thinking ahead so I didn't have to. We began to settle into a familiar pattern: Once we had arrived at the next city, Becky and I would have an early dinner at around 3:30 p.m. so I could digest it before the show, with very little conversation since I had to preserve my voice. Luckily Becky and I were both comfortable with companionable silence. We tried to find restaurants that were nonsmoking, but in certain parts of the country this was difficult because a restaurant's nonsmoking section would often be right next to a table in the smoking section with people just puffing away! Although I had smoked occasionally when I was a teenager, as an adult I had developed smoke allergies, and even a little exposure to it could wreak havoc on my vocal cords. Becky and I sometimes gave up trying to eat out and ordered room service instead.

There was no time for leisure or fun on the road for me. Sometimes the rest of the cast and crew would go out on the town after a show, and they often cajoled me to join them. "Come with us, Miss T!" they would say. "We heard about this amazing dance club and we're all going to check it out." But I had to refuse every time. I couldn't risk being stuck somewhere with cigarette smoke or relinquishing any of my energy on anything that wasn't *Victor/Victoria*. My entire life was devoted to making sure I would be able to perform the best show I could for the next audience who had paid good money to see it. Actually you could say that I lived like a nun for that entire tour.

As we had planned, Daryl flew out once every couple of weeks to stay with me. I would rather he had put our two dogs on the plane and sent them instead—they would have been far better company. To hell with the fact that I was the one pulling off eight strenuous performances every week; when Daryl arrived everything suddenly had to revolve around him and his needs. Becky would have to scramble to find a suitable restaurant that Daryl would approve of. And even though he was there physically I felt just as lonely as I did when he'd been away. I was always relieved when he finally left to go back home.

When I was in the midst of troubles that developed later, Mark Hoebee, our very wise director whom I came to admire tremendously, told me something that made me think.

"Toni," he'd said. "There are two kinds of actors who want to be on the road: the ones who look at the entire experience as one big traveling party, and the ones who are usually running away from something."

It wasn't long until I figured out which one I was.

CHAPTER 20

VICTOR/VICTORIA MADE ITS WAY FROM CITY TO CITY LIKE A TRAIN that never stopped. I had hoped that some of my anxiety would dissipate once we hit the road, but it didn't.

The stress had nothing to do with the actual show— I absolutely loved playing the role of Victoria. Being onstage allowed me to slip outside myself and leave all worries behind as I sang and danced through the delightful score with my "family" of cast mates. For those two hours I could forget Toni and just be Victoria, who was feisty and full of confidence and had a happily-ever-after life waiting when the curtain fell. I loved feeling the audience's emotions as the show progressed, hearing their laughter at the comic parts, and their thunderous applause at the end of a musical number.

Only when I was onstage in those last moments, holding hands with the cast while we took our final bows, would the dread of reality return. I'd try to keep my energy up for the usual round of meet-and-greets after each performance before rushing to my hotel room to shower, scrub off my stage makeup, and try to calm myself down so I could sleep. It would often be well into the wee hours by the time I actually did fall asleep. Then, before I knew it, morning would arrive and it was time for interviews or another day of travel.

I worried constantly about my voice. While I could do a pretty good job of avoiding cigarette smoke, there were other elements that affected my voice that I couldn't escape. Many of the theaters we performed in were very old, dating back to the vaudeville days, with heavy velvet curtains and upholstery filled with decades of dust. When you combine that with musty hotel rooms, dry, recirculated air in planes, constantly fluctuating weather conditions, and singing through eight shows a week, keeping a strong and healthy voice becomes a difficult task. Sometimes I felt as though I were tiptoeing through a minefield, trying to work around my swollen and overstressed vocal cords. Also, I was beginning to realize that my particular voice—usually so strong and trustworthy—was actually quite vulnerable. I feared that it might not be able to withstand the rigors of eight shows a week. And we were not even half way through the tour.

A thought began to haunt me as my vocal cords became more and more inflamed: *I had offered myself so confidently as a reliable leading lady for this production, but I was a fraud.* I began to wake up each morning with a sense of dread. *Would my voice do what I needed it to do tonight? Would I get up on the stage, in front of a packed audience, and not be able to sing?* I was absolutely terrified.

In order to save my vocal strength, I developed a strict routine of silence for most of the time that I was offstage. Upon waking, I would not speak a word. Then as the afternoon approached, I would cautiously begin to vocalize, slowly warming up for the evening show. All the while, I worried about those two little pieces of gristle, no larger than the lead of a pencil, that were my vocal cords. Often that tiny, stubborn instrument, upon which my whole career depended, would refuse to cooperate because of the allergens that seemed to be everywhere.

A few weeks into the tour, I experienced my first panic attack. We were in Grand Rapids, Michigan, and my hotel room was hermetically sealed, so I couldn't open the window even a crack for fresh air. As I began my vocal exercises, to warm up and prepare for the night's performance, I realized that the recirculating air through the ducts was blowing smoke from adjoining smoking rooms into my room. Phlegm was starting to build around my vocal cords, causing them to become inflamed. The more I worried about the upcoming performance, only hours away, the more panicked I became. I went outside for a walk along the river to calm down, but the weather was very cold and dry, and it only made me feel worse. My heart pounded so hard I could feel it in my ears. Riding the elevator back up to my room I felt like my entire throat was closing so tight that I couldn't breathe. I had the overwhelming urge to tear out of the hotel, hail a cab, and go straight to the airport for the next flight home.

Of course I could not do this. I was legally contracted to do the tour, and if I had quit, there was a very good chance that the show's producers could have sued me. I had no choice but to go on. With a few deep breaths, I made it back to my hotel room and began to prepare to leave for the venue. How I gathered the strength to make it through the performance that night, I will never know.

As we went from city to city, the anxiety began to overcome me again. I had very little appetite and would have to force myself to eat so I could have enough energy to do the show. But I still lost so much weight that my stage costumes began to hang on me like they would on a wire hanger. At night I would lie in bed trying to sleep, but my mind churned relentlessly. I knew that the rest of the cast and crew were depending on me, so I tried to hide how I was feeling and keep a cheerful face whenever I was around them.

Daryl would usually fly in for visits every other Monday and meet us in our new destination. Instead of being able to spend some quiet time settling into my hotel room before the week of performances ahead, Becky and I had to make sure that Daryl was satisfied with his lodgings and that his "healthy" meals were organized for the duration of his visit. He usually wasn't very interested in how I was feeling or anything having to do with the show, so our conversations, such as they were, centered around topics that Daryl wanted to discuss: the latest news he'd read online about the dangers of GMOs, or other food-related issues, or the many bizarre conspiracy theories he ascribed to. He knew that talking about these kinds of negative things drove me crazy, but I also think he knew they "pushed my buttons" and upset me, so he would continue his rants until I finally walked out of the room. The moment he left to fly back home I would breathe a sigh of relief. The heavy weight of his dark negativity was off my shoulders—until the next visit.

After I had been out on tour for a few weeks, Daryl called to tell me that he had bought a house in Las Vegas, over four hundred miles from our home in Washoe Valley, and would be living there until I returned from the tour.

"What?" I cried. "Daryl, why in the hell did you buy a house in Las Vegas?"

I found out later that this was something he had been planning to do all along once I left to go on tour. He hadn't even asked me, probably knowing that I would object. But even if I had objected, Daryl would have gone ahead and bought it anyway. In my mind, there was no reason for us to own a second house: we already *had* a huge, beautiful house. And even though Jennifer was living there while she cared for the pets, Daryl had the spacious guesthouse, which is where he had decided he wanted to stay, all to himself. And for a person who seldom left his room anyway, it should have been just fine. Thank goodness I knew that Jennifer would take care of Bodie, Adelaide, and the cats as though they were her own—Daryl obviously had no interest in doing so.

"I'm not staying out here while you're gone," was the only explanation that Daryl ever gave me. Why he even wanted a house in Las Vegas is beyond me—he didn't have any friends there, and he wouldn't have set foot inside a casino if his life had depended on it—but I guess he just cooked his health food and sat in front of the computer as he did at home. Because he must have known it would upset me, buying the house was probably a kind of punishment for my "leaving him behind" while I was away on tour.

Also startling was the *Love Boat* situation coming up all over again. Daryl told me after I had returned from the tour that he had considered Victoria's love scene with her romantic interest, King Marchand—which was really just a passionate embrace and a stage kiss—to be cheating on him. In Daryl's eyes, it was even worse than *Love Boat* because I had played the scene, and the kiss, for eight shows a week. The funny thing was I hadn't even particularly cared for the actor who had played King Marchand, but I was too drained to even argue with Daryl about it. It wouldn't have made any difference anyway.

When the show landed in Pittsburgh, I stayed in a lovely hotel suite with windows overlooking the confluence of the three rivers that run through the city, with a great view of the famed Three Rivers baseball stadium. As I relaxed before the show, enjoying the views, I was feeling pretty good. Then the phone rang. It was Jennifer from back home, bearing some heartbreaking news. One of our cats, George, had figured out a way to slip through the dog door late one night. He hadn't been seen since. I knew immediately that meant that he was probably dead, since coyotes and other predators roamed the land around our house. Indoor cats have very little chance of surviving the wilderness of Washoe Valley.

The news hit me hard. Of course, my immediate thought was that if I had been home, this would not have happened. George's death was all my fault. I was shattered; I cried for hours and slipped deeper into the perilous fathoms of a depression that had been looming for weeks. Dear Becky, my faithful road companion, did everything she could to comfort me, but after that day I was helplessly adrift in the seething tide of emotional despair. Anyone who has ever suffered a severe bout of depression knows that it can be impossible for a friend or loved one, no matter how well meaning, to pull you out of such a state. I got through the shows, but I was going downhill fast.

Despite my own emotional and voice-related troubles, there were some happy times on the tour. I adored my director, Mark Hoebee, and my family of young actors, singers, and dancers. I always kept an "open door" policy in my dressing room at the theater, so that any cast or crew member was welcome to come in and say hello, share a confidence, or ask for some advice—from their much, much older star! They would pass on a bit of gossip or share photos of their pets and loved ones from back home. I felt like I was a kind of "Mom" to these kids, and being with them helped me cast aside my own darkness for a while.

Many of the fans I met on the tour were wonderful as well. But sometimes I just had to laugh at what people perceived as the "glamorous life" of a star on tour, when reality is quite different. I remember one performance in Cincinnati. The show had gone beautifully and the audience was fantastic; they got all the jokes and responded with an enthusiastic standing ovation. At the finale, I appeared as Victoria in a spectacular gold gown, bowing to the applause with a genuine smile and appreciation for the audience. It was glorious, and I basked in the joy of the moment.

Two hours later, Becky and I found ourselves in the dim, and not particularly clean, hotel laundry facility, watching our socks and underwear go around and around in the soapy water. Glamour had nothing to do with it.

My breaking point came in Norfolk, Virginia. I had been struggling with my voice, and I was extremely on edge. People had warned us that the area of Norfolk where the theater was located could be dangerous and that we should be cautious in our comings and goings. When we arrived at the theater to prepare for the first show, I opened my dressing room door and found a strange man standing inside. He rushed toward me. "I'm a huge fan of yours, Miss Tennille!" he exclaimed, with his arms held out. "And I've been dying to talk to you!" I immediately backed out of the door and ran to find security, and they quickly removed the man from the theater.

Later, I learned that he was the same man who had been stalking me by email for some time. No one could figure out how he had slipped past security to get into my dressing room. The theater staff assured me that extra personnel would be posted for my protection. But the anxiety of fearing for my personal safety, along with all my other concerns, was the final straw. After that incident, every negative thing that happened to me burned like electric shocks through my overstressed psyche. Daryl arrived for a visit, which only added to my stress.

I was in desperate need of a reality check. A friend suggested I contact Betty Buckley, the great Tony Award–winning Broadway star, to ask her for some advice on how she survived through her long years of touring. I had seen Betty on Broadway in the lead role in *Sunset Boulevard*, and her brilliant performance had blown me away. When I phoned Betty, she was full of wisdom— unfortunately, most of it was too late in my case. For example, she told me that, before signing any contract, I should have insisted that an understudy perform my role in all of the matinee shows. This would cut the number of shows I had to do every week from eight to six and allow a lot more time for rest and recuperation. Betty was so incredibly kind to me, and even offered to fly to Norfolk for a visit to lend her support. But I thanked her, insisting that although I greatly appreciated her generous offer, I was fine and could manage on my own.

But I wasn't fine. I was by now so mired in depression I could hardly speak, and I made the decision that I was going to go home. Becky arranged flights for me, Daryl, and herself, informed the stage manager that I was ill and needed to go home for a while, and we left Norfolk and flew home that very night. My understudy would play the role of Victoria while I was gone.

The day after we arrived home to Washoe Valley, my doctor admitted me to the local hospital for what he called "dehydration." Complete emotional collapse is what I called it. I stayed in the hospital for a couple of days, sleeping almost the entire time. When I was discharged, I made an appointment with a cognitive therapist, Daniel Dugan, who had been highly recommended. With Daniel's help I began to find my way back to myself, and even to see the possibility that I might be able to rejoin the tour. Another element was crucial in my healing, one that I had resisted for a long time: antidepressant medication.

Jane, who is an RN in Florida, had been in regular contact with me as I had started my emotional decline while on the road. She encouraged me to give antidepressants a try. Jane had seen them help others and felt that the meds could go a long way in helping me cope for the rest of the tour. And, if I wanted to stop once the tour was over and I was back home, I could. So, my doctor prescribed Prozac and I duly began taking it. My doctor also told me it would take a few weeks for the drug to start working, and not to expect anything right away. Jane had taken time off from work to accompany me for some of the tour stops, and her comforting, supportive presence was balm to my spirits.

When I rejoined the tour in New Orleans, I could tell the rest of the cast and crew were covertly watching for signs that I might not really be ready to come back, but they were all kind and encouraging. And once they saw that I *was* back and ready to work hard and put on a great show, we resumed the tour as the family we had been from the start.

When Jane left New Orleans to fly home, I sobbed like a baby as I watched her wave good-bye and disappear into the crowd at the airport. But I would be seeing her again soon, when the show played in Orlando, and I knew she was only a phone call away. She also said she would join me later on the tour to celebrate our final performance in Cleveland.

Victor/Victoria went to Florida, and my dear friend Dotty Lienau flew out from Reno to join me in Tampa. It did my heart good to have her there. From Tampa we went to Miami. I had been waiting for the Prozac to kick in ever since I had started it, but I hadn't felt any lifting of the darkness that still surrounded me. Then, one day in Miami, as I took an early morning walk on the beach, I suddenly felt like a light had switched on in my head. Everything would be all right, I realized at that moment.

And I experienced a glimmer of happiness—the first one in many months!

This feeling waxed and waned for a few days, and then, gradually, it began to stay with me for longer and longer durations. I could actually feel joy flow back through me. I knew then that I could finish the tour . . . and that I might actually enjoy it! When the tour finally came to a close, forty weeks after it had begun, I was overcome with emotion. But this time it was a good emotion.

We played the last performance of *Victor/Victoria* in Cleveland, where Jane again joined us for the final shows. I found Cleveland to be a welcoming, progressive city and a virtual oasis of the arts in all forms. People packed the theater, and their applause was thunderous. I took my last bow with a sense of pride for what the cast and I had accomplished, through the good and the bad.

Right after the final show, Daryl, who had flown in for the closing performance, and I played a private Captain and Tennille concert for the cast and crew—the first in many years—and it was so much fun. When we all said good-bye, there were so many hugs and tears I hardly made it through with my mascara intact. I *had* made it through, though, and I was finally going home.

There were many lessons I learned from my experience with *Victor/Victoria*. The most important was that I learned I am not the tough, strong woman I always thought I was. I needed help, and I got it—from my friends and family, the cast and crew of the show who had suffered through the hard times with me, and, yes, from professionals in the medical field. But most crucial was that I had allowed myself to ask for the help I needed, and when it was offered, I took it. None of us is made of steel . . . we are all flesh-and-blood human beings, flawed and full of self-doubt, capable of both intense sadness and rapturous joy. And we really do need each other.

CHAPTER 21

When we were in our late sixties, Daryl and I decided we needed to move to a location where the winters didn't produce the six or more feet of snow that Washoe Valley got. We knew that having to shovel and plow all that snow would become more and more difficult as we grew older. Some friends of mine had suggested that we take a look at Prescott, Arizona. When I researched online, I learned the area had four distinct seasons, but none was extreme. It sounded exactly like what we were looking for.

Prescott is a small community about two hours north of Phoenix in the high desert plains of Arizona. In 2007, we bought two acres in a scenic, rural development called American Ranch with spectacular views of the seven-thousand-feet-high Granite Mountain. Here, we planned to build our very last home. Daryl hunkered down to design the house, as he had with our previous two homes. And, as before, the house became far bigger than what the two of us needed. Daryl kept adding more square footage to the plans, and very soon we had exceeded the budget we had both agreed upon.

While waiting for the house to be built, we rented a small home nearby. As I was walking my two Australian Shepherds, Hubble and Adelaide, through the neighborhood, I met a woman whom I saw regularly walking her own two Aussies. We became friends, and soon after, she took me to meet Kathy Bryan of Redrock Aussies. Kathy, who is an Australian Shepherd "Hall of Fame" breeder, is highly selective and does not breed her dogs often. But the day we met she happened to have a litter of ten beautiful, two-week old puppies. Not long after, when Daryl and I moved into our newly completed house, Kathy gave me one of those puppies, and he became my special boy, Smoky.

I'd already been an avid fan of the breed, and had done quite a bit of hiking with my own dogs, but Kathy introduced me to a whole new world of Aussies. She became my guide into the wonderful sport of canine agility, and she also got me interested in the Pet Partners therapy program at our local hospital. Smoky, with his calm demeanor and sweet nature, became a beloved and comforting presence there, just as his sire Moon had been before him with Kathy.

Australian Shepherds are smart, versatile, beautiful dogs, and they have a natural talent for canine agility. The sport combines so many of the things I love: dogs, physical activity, and social inter-action. It wasn't long until I became immersed in the energetic and happy world of agility enthusiasts.

While I was busy practicing with the dogs, traveling to agility and conformation trials, and doing my canine therapy work at the hospital, my relationship with Daryl continued to be the same kind of odd, distant cohabitation we'd had for years. Although he had a few friends from back in his music days that he was still in contact with, he only communicated with them by email or phone and never wanted to see them in person. I tried to encour-age him to spend time with his friends, because socializing is so beneficial for a person's health, but he didn't listen.

Daryl spent most of his time alone in his room at our home in Prescott. When he designed the house, he had included a vast net-work of intercom systems that enabled communication between each room. With a push of the button, Daryl could "summon" me, entreating me to bring him something to eat, or to search through the many files he kept near his bed for some document he'd mis-placed. The problem was that Daryl was perfectly capable, with a little extra effort, of walking to the kitchen and getting his own yogurt. But I'd always drop whatever I was doing and do as he asked. Why did I acquiesce to his every demand, even if it meant interrupting my own life numerous times a day? I suppose that all those decades that Daryl and I had been together had "conditioned" me to do what he asked. So, to prevent the inevitable complaints and negativity that would result if I refused, I just did as he wished.

Back when we still lived in Washoe Valley, Daryl began to be alarmed by the trembling in his hands and the shaking he would experience during his occasional panic attacks. After he was examined by a neurologist in Reno, the doctor said it could be the symptom of a number of things, from stress to familial tremors to, possibly, Parkinson's disease. He suggested we go to California to have Daryl examined by the chief neurologist at Stanford Medical Center. But once the Reno neurologist had mentioned Parkinson's disease, that was the only word Daryl could hear.

Daryl was so panicked by the idea he might have Parkinson's that, when I tried to calm him down a bit while we were on our way to Stanford, he lashed out at me, cursing as I tried to navigate the unfamiliar highway. The next day, after a battery of tests, the neurologist told us she was certain that Daryl did not have Parkinson's. But her diagnosis did nothing to ease Daryl's fear. He was convinced that he had the disease.

Once we moved to Arizona, Daryl saw several other neurologists, one of whom said that in his opinion, Daryl did have Parkinson's. A second physician wasn't sure she agreed with that diagnosis, and a third said that in his opinion Daryl did not have Parkinson's but some other neurological condition and he wanted to do more tests, but Daryl refused.

Despite being given a clean bill of health by the chief of neurology at the famed Stanford Medical Center, along with other specialists, Daryl plunged into the role of someone suffering from a chronic illness. More boxes of supplements and "cures" arrived every week, although Daryl often decided after using them for a week or two that they didn't work and would throw the rest away. He might as well have been withdrawing money from the bank and setting it on fire.

A little over a year after we moved to Prescott, Daryl had replacement surgery on both of his knees at the same time, even though our doctor had recommended he do one knee at a time. He also refused to complete the postsurgery physical therapy that was crucial to healing his knees and strengthening his muscles. The intercom buzzer rang incessantly, making me cringe every time I heard Daryl's voice through the speaker. Every day, I had to go into his room to retrieve and empty the urine container that he kept next to his bed, even though he was by that time capable of getting up and going to the bathroom himself. Finally, I'd had enough and told him I wasn't going to empty his urine bottle anymore. Realizing that I meant what I said, he did it himself for a short while. But eventually, we hired someone to attend to Daryl, although even this upset me, because I strongly believed that it would benefit him to do some things for himself. As a result, the longer Daryl stayed in bed, the more atrophied his muscles became.

When we had lived in Nevada, Daryl had begun to delve into the netherworld of the Internet and all its conspiratorial trappings. He spent hours reading up on his favorite topics: health food and supplements, various diseases, and the many "miraculous" remedies that could cure all of his symptoms. With practically all the information in the world available online—some legit, some not— Daryl began to diagnose himself with a variety of ailments.

"I can't eat that type of bread anymore," he told me one day as I pulled out his usual organic variety from the grocery bag. "It's not good for my Extended Left Arm Syndrome."

"Daryl," I sighed. "What exactly is Extended Left Arm Syndrome?"

I shouldn't even have asked. Over the next few years, Daryl changed his "food rules" on a regular basis. One day he decided that it was the yogurt that was causing him to see flashing lights that would cross his vision from time to time, and he abruptly stopped eating it. Yogurt was a food Daryl had eaten, and actually enjoyed, ever since I'd known him. It turned out that Daryl had a medical condition called "silent migraine." Those afflicted with this condition can experience the "aura" that heralds the onset of a migraine headache, but they do not suffer the excruciating pain itself. This was not a serious condition and Daryl was fortunate: In its various forms the "aura" can be a nuisance but nothing like what real migraine sufferers go through. Despite this minor ailment our family doctor had declared that Daryl was physically one of the healthiest patients in his practice. Amazingly this did not seem to be the news that Daryl wanted to hear, but after a few weeks he grudgingly conceded that yogurt was safe and began to eat it again.

Daryl continued to devote endless hours to his "research" and constantly scanned his body for symptoms of disease. One day he told me that he was suffering from something called "Mad Tongue Disease." Wearily, I suggested that perhaps he should again visit our general practitioner, who had patiently dealt with Daryl and his hypochondria for years, to see what he thought. But what the doctor said wouldn't have mattered to Daryl anyway. And of course, where there's a medical issue, there are a thousand quacks out there eager to sell you something to cure it. Packages from around the world regularly arrived on our doorstep, often stinking of pungent herbs or oils right through the box. When I found out that many of these "medicines" cost thousands of dollars, I begged Daryl to have some sense and to stop believing everything he read on the Internet. My efforts to reason with him were in vain. But the cracks in my patience, which had been solid for so many years, began to show.

One night I was preparing a salad, with all of the usual "Daryl-approved" ingredients, for dinner. When I turned away for a moment, Smoky, who had been observing from the floor, put his front paws up on the counter and snatched a mouthful of lettuce from the bowl.

"Smoky, no!" I cried as he wandered off with his prize. With a heavy sigh, I began to pick up the bowl to throw the salad away and start preparing a fresh one. Even though Smoky had only grabbed a small mouthful and had not touched the rest, this was a "tainted" salad and Daryl would refuse to eat it.

But then, as I held the bowl over the garbage, a thought came to me. *Daryl would never know.* The revelation gave me pause. *If you don't* say *anything, he'll never know!* So, I put a large helping of the salad on each of our plates, set one on Daryl's dinner tray, and carried it to his room. When I went back later to retrieve the tray, I saw that he had eaten every bite of the salad, and a glimmer of rebellion began to germinate. It felt really good.

When we moved to Prescott, I had made up my mind to retire from touring. I wanted to lead a more normal life, and not having to worry about my voice any more was an absolute relief. I did perform three concerts, one per year, as a kind of gift to the people of Prescott, who had so enthusiastically welcomed me to their community. But other than that, I was done with public life.

It was during those years that I finally gave up trying to "break through" to Daryl. Over the decades of our marriage, I had tried so many different approaches to acquire even a minimal amount of intimacy with him. There had been the many, many songs that I had written for, and about, him, songs whose lyrics expressed my love and yearning. I found out years later that Daryl never paid any attention to what the lyrics meant—all he cared about was the music. There had also been the countless times of "protecting" Daryl from situations I knew he wouldn't like, making excuses for his standoffish behavior toward others. I had even tried more practical approaches; some that I gleaned from books about psychology and the like. One of these attempts was "The Golden Hour."

Daryl had the habit of starting every day with some kind of negative comment or incendiary statement, usually about something he had heard the night before on one of his "conspiracy" radio programs. I hated to start my day in such a manner. Finally, I suggested that we enact what I called "The Golden Hour," where neither of us would say anything negative within the first hour after waking. Daryl was absolutely unable to go longer than ten minutes before starting in again on his theories about why, in his opinion, the entire world was going to hell in a handbasket. "The Golden Hour" was not going to work with Daryl, and that was the end of that.

I could spend a lifetime trying to figure out why Daryl Dragon was the way he was. If I think back to some of the stories Daryl had told me about his life, a kind of pattern emerges like a faint path through an overgrown wood. There is Daryl when he was a little boy, watching his mother, Eloise, suffer a severe mental breakdown when the family was traveling back home from Europe on an ocean liner. Later, an adolescent Daryl had to endure the pain of seeing his mother turn into an almost robotic figure after she underwent a prefrontal lobotomy in a botched effort to cure her bipolar disorder. In later years, with her condition most likely worsened by the surgeon's knife, Eloise's demons intensified. Although Daryl's mother loved him unconditionally, she just couldn't be there for him. Tortured by dreadful mood swings and deep depression, Eloise took to her bed, and there she stayed for the remainder of her life.

Meanwhile Daryl's father, Carmen, the dashing, handsome, and famous composer and conductor, criticized his children relentlessly and many times even struck them for no apparent reason. I remember going over to Daryl's parents' house after we'd just met. Carmen was tanning himself on the patio of their Malibu home, his muscular body coated in oil as he held a foil magnifier to his face, while Eloise, the woman who had once had the voice of an angel, lay alone and silent inside the dark house.

This kind of childhood surely had a devastating effect on a sensitive boy like Daryl. Each of Daryl's four siblings, two brothers and two sisters, bore, in his or her own way, the scars from their traumatic upbringing. Kathy, the baby of the family and a talented flutist, had been a creative, fragile soul who never overcame the family curse of depression. Kathy had adored Daryl since they were children, and whenever I saw them together, I could see that she wasn't getting the love she craved so much from her older brother. In 2012, Kathy tragically took her own life. Daryl never cried when we learned about her death, although if he mourned for his sister when he was alone I will never know. He didn't attend her funeral, and rarely spoke of her again afterward.

Trying to imagine what kind of man Daryl might have been without a childhood full of emotional turmoil and abuse was futile. My own parents might have been less than perfect, but even through the hardest of times, I always knew that they loved me. Believing that love could heal anything, I had tried for so long to break through to Daryl, but the damage had already been done. I was a lifetime too late.

And there was still my own life to consider. I had spent so many of my adult years desperately trying to make Daryl happy, while at the same time, denying it to myself. When I turned seventy, I was lucky enough to be active, strong, and still up for adventure. With my wonderful friends and my beloved Aussies, I'd found a new purpose in life. As long as my heart beat in my chest, there was still hope for me to try to find my own happiness. Even if it meant I had to kick and tear my way out of that circle of control Daryl had drawn, I had to do it. The thought was always there, lingering, but it would take a few more years before I actually had the courage to break free.

After we had been in our American Ranch home for a few years, we received an alarming call from our financial manager. He informed us that we were spending far too much money on the upkeep of our huge house, and if we didn't make some changes, we'd be out of money in a few years. This was the first time I realized that, despite all our years of hard work, we could possibly lose everything. I was stunned.

I knew we had to sell the house immediately and downsize to something more manageable. But when we had bought our property and built the house, the real estate market had been on an upswing. Now it was down, and we had a very difficult time selling it, because the market for a house the size and price of ours was almost nil. We did finally sell it, but ended up taking a huge loss.

Our next house in Prescott was still spacious, but not nearly as large as the one we'd sold. It had all the room Daryl required to store all of his stuff, which, he explained to me, would save us money because we would not have to rent a storage space. While we were settling into our new house, Daryl decided we needed a generator. He had begun to become increasingly paranoid about something he'd read on the Internet, a supposed "theory" that the government would end up stealing everyone's electricity. Therefore, he told me, we needed to be prepared for when that time came.

One rainy, cold night in January, Daryl called me to his room. "Here's the generator we need," he said, holding up his laptop to show me. This particular generator was strong enough to power a small city, and it cost almost $10,000.

"Daryl, no." I said. "Absolutely not. We can't afford that . . . and we don't need it!"

"Too late!" he retorted, slamming the laptop shut. "I've already ordered it!"

"We can't afford this right now." I said quietly, "You have to cancel the order."

"Get out, you fucking bitch!" Daryl screamed, pointing toward the hallway.

I was so stunned that I just stood there. Daryl and I had had our differences for many years, but he had never cursed at me with such rage. Perhaps he had his own reasons to be angry, reasons I could never understand even though I had tried repeatedly. Maybe I had unwittingly done something to evoke this vitriolic response. But at that moment, I knew that I had no choice but to leave our marriage.

I backed out and softly closed the door. I felt suddenly awakened, as if I had been reborn, my eyes opening to the world for the first time. Even though I'd never truly known Daryl despite all the years we had been together, the person who had cursed me from his bed, with those furiously burning eyes, was a man who was completely beyond my reach. I had tried to save him for so long; now it was time to save myself.

A few days later, I filed for divorce.

After I filed for divorce, I bought my very own little house near Granite Mountain, taking my three Aussies and two cats with me. Life took on an easy, relaxed routine, and I filled my days with friends, agility trials, and canine therapy work at the hospital. My sister Louisa and her husband Bob moved to Prescott from California, which delighted me. Louisa also quickly became enchanted with Australian Shepherds and developed into a talented and dedicated agility handler with her own three Aussies. Louisa never fails to make me laugh with her razor-sharp wit and wry observations; having her and Bob so near was wonderful. Daryl moved into a comfortable cottage home of his own, in an adult-living community on the other side of Prescott. He has people to help anytime he needs it. We speak occasionally, and despite everything, I do care about him and wish him well.

News of the divorce brought a wave of nasty publicity. "Evil Tennille leaves disabled Captain," was one particularly ugly headline. Another article trumpeted that I now lived in a "luxurious mansion" while Daryl subsisted in a hovel. That one was especially funny, as my new house was quite modest. I refused to speak to the press after the divorce, despite their sneaking around to take pictures of me in my backyard or knocking on my door, so they simply filled in the blanks themselves.

The media quickly moved onto someone else, and I was finally left alone. But even though I was happy in my little house with my dogs and cats, I couldn't shake the feeling that something was missing. A kind of tugging deep inside that said, "Hey, this isn't your last gig, you know!" I wasn't sure what it meant, but despite my newfound peace, there still lingered a small doubt that I would spend the rest of my life in Prescott. I was also concerned about possibly having to ask Louisa for help as I grew older, because she is much younger than I am and has her own busy life. I despaired at the thought of being a burden on her, or anyone else.

Then one night, Jane called.

"There's something I want to talk to you about," she said. "I have been thinking about it for a while. Now, I want you to hear me out . . . and you can't say *anything* until I am done speaking."

"OK . . ."

I held my breath, and Jane continued. "I want you to think about moving to Florida." And she went on to explain that as we both got older, it was important to be closer to each other. Jane is not quite two years younger than I, so we share a similar path through our "golden years." She continued, "Toni, you and I can help each other and have a great time together, but not if we are thousands of miles apart. Come live in Florida so we can see each other every day, not just twice a year."

It took me less than twenty-four hours to decide. Actually, I knew the moment Jane said it that it was exactly what I needed to do. I called her back the very next day. "I'm going to do it. I'm moving to Florida!"

Before the month was up, I had my Prescott house on the market. Jane scouted around for a house that I could buy close to hers and sent me regular pictures and updates. Then one day she called: "I found it." The photos Jane sent showed a lovely gabled yellow house trimmed in white—just large enough for me and the dogs. As I stared at the picture of the house, I felt tears come to my eyes. I was going home.

THE END

EPILOGUE

It is now late November of 2015, and I have been living in Florida for over three wonderful months. When Jane had called to tell me about the house she discovered, she had said, "Toni, it is perfect for you."

And perfect it is! The modestly sized house is set cozily among pine trees, oaks veiled in Spanish moss, and thick hedges of green foliage. It has a classic design with stone accents and four peaked gables. To top it all off, it sits in a quiet neighborhood a mere two miles from where Jane and my brother-in-law Frank live.

Barely a month after Jane called about my moving to Florida I had packed up all my belongings and shipped them east. Then, with my dear friend Carol Sutton to help with driving and wrangling of my three rambunctious Aussies, we drove the 2,500 miles from Arizona to Florida. It took us four and a half days to make the trip but thanks to Carol, it felt more like an adventure than a hassle. Once we arrived, the dogs took immediately to the roomy backyard, racing happily among the trees and ferns. Here in Florida there is never a shortage of lizards or squirrels for them to chase (fortunately, they never actually catch anything) so every moment in their yard is full of excitement. I fell into the warm embrace of my East Coast family—Jane, Frank, Caroline, and their wonderful friend Marie Cranmer, who is now a dear friend of mine. They did more than I ever could have dreamed to help me settle in and feel welcome.

For those of you who are concerned about Daryl, he is actually doing well. He and I chat on the phone every couple of weeks and he sounds stronger than I have heard him in a very long time. It makes me think that the divorce was not only good for me, but possibly good for him as well.

I'm still making the transition to my new home, but never once have I doubted my decision to come to Florida. I love my sweet, simple house more than any of the enormous, custom-built homes Daryl and I ever had. Most late afternoons I find myself sitting on my screened porch—which they call a "Florida room" here—with my dogs, and perhaps a nice glass of wine, savoring the end of another beautiful day.

How very blessed I am.

Acknowledgments

To our agent, Jennifer Di Chiara, who believed in us from the very beginning.

To our publisher, Rowman & Littlefield/Taylor Trade, editor Rick Rinehart, Jessica Kastner, Meredith Dias, Sara Given, Evan Helmlinger, and the rest of the Taylor staff, who saw merit in our work and have given this fledgling team their full help and support.

To Judy Donaldson, who lent her keen editing skills during the early stages.

To Jamie Blaine, who advised and encouraged us through his own experiences as a published writer.

To TEAM DAISY: Jane Tennille, Frank Engs, Marie Cranmer, and Michael Donaldson, all of whom have given their love and support throughout this entire project (and who have given us many laughs too).

And to my sisters: Jane, Louisa, and Melissa, who helped sharpen my focus when some of my memories were a bit fuzzy around the edges.